# Network Marketing
# STRAIGHT TALK

## By

## George Zalucki

ISBN 978-0-615-22168-7

PRINTED IN THE UNITED STATES OF AMERICA

Visit
www.georgezalucki.com
for more information about George Zalucki!
Visit The George Zalucki Store to
purchase many other motivational
products on CD and DVD!

# "What kind of business would my business be, if everyone in it, worked just like me?"

" We all have the capacity for radical transformation and the cost of awareness is responsibility."

"The evidence of responsibility is a commitment to personal growth and living one's life at "cause" rather than "effect."

*George Zalucki*

Ask yourself, everyday,
"Is what I am about to
do, moment by moment,
leading me toward my
objective, or away from my
objective, and pick!"

"You have a responsibility
to become all you are
capable of becoming
in this journey called
life or I see no valid
intellectual or spiritual
reason for existence. Too
many people wake up in

the morning and don't even know why they are getting out of bed other than to survive. People get out of bed one of two ways. You need to decide which one you are . You are either "inspired" or "not inspired"; pick one! Because if you don't shape your world with passion, this world will hardly notice you were here."

# *Contents*

## Section 3 – Critical Insights for Success     119

## Section 4 - Articles To Encourage You     131

## Section 5 – The Summary     191

## Section 6 – The Workbook     21

# *Introduction To The Author*

George Zalucki is considered among the very best personal development trainers in the world today. His adroit style of communicating has captured his listening and reading audiences, compelling them to look closely at what really stops them from getting what they want out of life.

George is a former college dean, teacher of Psychology, Sociology and counselor. He was a corporate VP of a Network Marketing company based in Dallas, TX. He has been an Independent Representative for 33 years, rising to the top of several companies. He has built large organizational sales teams of over 100,000 distributors in 21 countries. His sales volume has exceeded $20 million per month, while earning millions of dollars in Network Marketing. He has been a consultant in the industry, and the keynote speaker at many national and international conventions.

George has been featured in Success From Home magazine, Chicken Soup For the Network Marketing Soul, Personal Excellence, and has been quoted in Hansard's, "The Official Record of the British Parliament," and referred to as a great American Philosopher by one of its members. George has been lecturing on what it takes to be a champion for 30 plus years in 21 countries and 3 continents.

The effects of his influence have reached many levels, including sport teams. One such example is the many times he is referred to in "Kicking Down Heavens Door" by Mickey Harte, who was the manager of the Irish soccer team that won the All-Ireland Championship in 2003. Mickey used many of George's teachings to coach his team to victory, especially his teachings on persistence and what it takes to achieve lofty dreams.

Many people have written to George over the years, thanking him for his teachings and for helping them to achieve success in business, both traditional and Network Marketing. Below are two such letters.

*Dear George,*
*I was recently honored to be a 2004 Marketing Executive of the Year with my company. I want to thank you for inspiring me to this level of achievement. You have been a friend, mentor, and a truly wonderful role model of success to me since we met in 1992. At my first "Experience To Make A Difference" Seminar I was broke financially, spiritually, and emotionally. I was hurt by the recent failure of my Real Estate business and was at the rock bottom place of my life. Your advice to me that day moved me to become a devoted student. I hung on every word and committed ALL your audio material to memory until they became a part of my very essence. Thank you for caring about me. You have been my inspiration and taught me we are already perfect beings and that everything is possible in this beautiful life. George, you are the best friend and mentor that could have ever come into my life.*

*Paul Kenny*
*Royal Ambassador*

*April 6, 2003*

*Dear George,*
*I was moved very deeply by the profound truths you presented at your powerful presentation today in London, England. In just one hour you touched me at a deep level and re-inspired me to change NOW and to take control of my life again at a challenging time in my life.*
*You are the best personal development speaker I have ever seen.*
*I have attended Anthony Robbins' "Unleash The Power Within," done the fire walk, and made many major changes in my life. Tony is a great person, he is inspiring. I am making a recovery from Chronic Fatigue Syndrome after attending his seminar.*
*You are phenomenal! You have a deep wisdom, spirituality, experience and maturity I have not seen in any other speaker and that makes you outstanding; you have truly arrived; you are truly enlightened and you really care about people.*
*I admire you for your success and achievement, and for your humility, compassion and empowerment of others. This is a sign of a true master.*
*You are the best! Thank you for the value you have added to my life and for talking to me personally and with so much understanding and love. The hug from you was great! It will be a day I treasure always, and your powerful words are carved in my mind. Wishing you the best in life.*
*Love, Joy, and Peace*
*Bano*

It is my sincere desire that this book will prove to be a valuable guide, assisting <u>you</u> to reach your dreams in Network Marketing and your personal life.

*George Zalucki*

# *Acknowledgements*

 I am excited for this opportunity to share with you the insights I've gained over the years in this industry. I thank the many teachers whose generosity of mind provided me the insights that herein flow from my mind to yours.

I count myself privileged to have been in the industry of Network Marketing for some 33 years. I have seen the Industry grow and change from a small business mentality into a very viable big business mentality, one that can change an average person's life and fortune to whatever he or she desires. I have been teaching the concepts of Success and the Principles of Human Achievement to Network Marketing audiences for many years. I have been in front of hundreds of thousands of persons in the United States, Canada, 19 countries in Europe, and soon in Africa for the people of the USSR and ex CIS Countries. Being able to help "Make A Difference" in a person's life both economically and personally is in itself a privilege I treasure. I trust this book will aid you on your path to Success!

I would like to thank the many people throughout the years who have encouraged me to put my teachings in writing, and especially my wife, Eloise, for her tremendous support in this endeavor.

# ***The Prologue***

Let's be straightforward and clear from the beginning! You are the only one that can add commitment and action to the ideas that follow. The ideas are proven. It's up to you to master the lessons and put them to work for you. A solid commitment can change your life. Commitment and action are invigorating, not fatiguing. I teach my audiences around the world a simple concept, ***"Commitment is doing the thing you said you would do, long after the mood you said it in has left you!"***

When you start a network marketing business, you are starting into business for yourself. There will be no one watching you punch a time clock. No one will know if you are making phone calls, setting up appointments, or just watching TV. So, you will have to keep your word to yourself and your commitment to succeed. This is a very important insight and the cornerstone teaching of the "Principles of Human Achievement". Keep Your Word! It sounds quite simple. However, it is amazing to observe the many people who do not keep their word to themselves and therefore they fail.

This book is all about <u>YOU!</u> You do not need someone telling you this is good information. You will recognize it when you read the pages. I have spoken these truths in front of hundred's of thousands of people throughout the years. Countless people have already validated the principles in this book with the results they have achieved in their lives. They have direct experience of the power of these principles to make a difference in their lives for the better.

As you read on you will realize that this book is for anyone seeking to better their lives. It is not just for the people seeking financial success. This book is for YOU no matter what your position in life. My hope is that many people that have never read a book on self-development will pick this up, read it seriously, and then apply these principles into their lives. These words are for you whether you are a laborer or a professional. This book and its message will help the mom at home raising her children, the high level corporate executive, as well as the retired person and the aspiring teenager.

I promise you will not need anyone convincing you that these Principles will work in your life. The word educate literally means "to lead or bring out". This implies that you already know the information. You need to bring it out to a higher state of awareness. Certain principles or teachings will give you a proverbial "Clunk" with your soul. That "clunk" or jolt is telling you which are the most needed principles for you to work on in your life. They are the ones that will make the biggest difference in your life circumstances. Some of these principles you may already be practicing in your life and that is good. However, you need every one of them to be truly successful and balanced.

The fact that you are reading these pages proves that you are interested in personal and financial growth. To realize a profit from this book, you will need two basic qualities:

1. *A sincere willingness to experience the truth; the truth about how your activities align with your intentions. No more excuses!*
2. *A willingness to take responsibility for your own success by doing what needs to be done. No more excuses!*

In building anything we need a plan and tools. Don't

allow yourself to be fooled by the brevity of this publication. It is directly to the point! It is designed to assist you personally and financially and to be a reference book for you to reflect on and evaluate your progress. The ideas here are not untested or vague theories. They are proven insights that work for everyone that applies them. May they contribute to your prosperity and happiness. Keep this book with you at all times. When you are disappointed with a prospect, meeting or outcome, read one of the chapters to encourage you! And, it will!!! Let's get started!

This book is divided into 4 sections. **Section 1** – The Basics provides information for the new Networker with insights for the experienced Networker, too. It will give you a new way to conceptualize Network Marketing and teach you some new ways to communicate it to others, i.e. sponsoring. **Section 2** – Psychological Insights is about understanding people, which is critical to recruiting, teaching, and motivating your team members. **Section 3** – Critical Insights will give you detailed success principles. An, **Section 4** – Articles To Encourage You are just that. Refer to them often.

**Section 5**- The summary is one of the most important parts of this book. What I have taught you in previous chapters all comes together for you. Read this many times!

Then, finally, at the end of this book is **Section 6** – The Workbook. Objective: To establish your primary reason for being involved in your Network Marketing business and determine your personal growth and income goals. You need to start by taking an honest personal inventory of your life, your assets and your liabilities, and then compare where you are now and where it is you want to be and by when   This is a very personal part of this publication. You will have an opportunity to rate your leadership abilities, write down your goals, and decide for yourself what is stopping you from reaching your goals. You see until you identify what is stopping you, it is impossible to overcome it. Then, you will identify your motivators and de-motivators. This section will provide clarity on how you measure up in several areas. You will see the areas that need improvement with clarity. It will be up to you to do the improving. No one else can do that for you. So, do the work required by you and on you and you can expect to see great results!

The subject of taxes has been left out of this book because it will be read by people in many countries, so I encourage you to seek the counsel of your tax authorities on what is allowed legally for tax advantages in owning your own business. It is an important ingredient of business to have an accurate understanding of your tax laws.

# Section I
# The Basics Of
# Network
# Marketing

# *Chapter 1 - What Is Network Marketing?*

Network Marketing is also commonly referred to as Multi-level Marketing or Relationship Marketing. It is a means of distribution that involves products and/or services and a compensation plan. When you join a network marketing company, you have just become the CEO and President of your own company. It is a very powerful means for the average person to earn extra or extra-ordinary income!

**Understanding the power of multiplication is the key to understanding your Network Marketing business and it's potential.**

Who makes more money - the owner of a McDonald's hamburger store or the owner who sells McDonald hamburger franchises? It's easy to see who makes more money in this situation. A very important statement was made by J. Paul Getty. He said, "The key to wealth is not to have a 100% of the best man, but rather to have 1% of 100 men."

Too few people in Network Marketing who are compensated by a multi-level compensation plan truly understand the principle and power of compounding. If they did, they would go to work! Let me give you an example. If you were to put a penny in a savings account that doubled everyday, by the end of a week you'd have 64 cents. At this point, unless you could see the potential of staying with the investment, you might conclude that 64 cents is not much money. But, by the end of the second week, you would have $40.96, and by the end of the third week, over $20,000. Would you believe that at the end of a month, you would have over 5 million dollars?!

This is the principle that Network Marketing income is based upon. You must decide if you will "run a store" or build a "franchise network"; whether your personal effort accounts for 100% of your income or whether 10 productive, self-motivated leaders account for 90% of your income.

The people who earn large incomes in this business learned to sell the products. But, they also learned how to encourage and motivate others to join their network as Independent Business Builders, thereby building platforms of distribution. Sponsoring business builders creates the power of compounding, which is THE PRINCIPLE upon which all wealth is built. Instead of 10 to 20 hours per week of work contributing to your income (you doing it alone), you would have hundreds of hours of sales and sponsoring efforts contributing to your wealth through your network of independent representatives. Representatives who dedicate themselves to developing and learning how to sponsor, motivate, and train others in Network Marketing, if successful at it, can build incomes that would be the envy of most corporate executives!!!

So look seriously at your Network Marketing opportunity. Involve yourself with a product line that you believe in! Be very familiar with the marketplace and your product. Be excited!

Here is your job description:

1. Get people to buy your product or service and also become a customer yourself.
2. Sponsor people that are looking for an income producing business and have them become a part of your network.

Or, more simply

1. Getting customers
2. Getting customer getters, who are your business builders.

**And remember, people move for their own reasons! Not yours or mine.** You need to present your opportunity attractively enough for your prospects to discover their <u>reasons</u> and <u>benefits</u> for joining you.

Your job is to provide powerful, factual information to stimulate interest.

When you build an organization, you will have taken the limits off time and physical capacity by expanding your efforts, by multiplying your efforts through others. This is exactly what large corporations do! However, you have the potential in Network Marketing to have a large network and yet no employees, no buildings, no account offices, and no headaches that come along with traditional business! Plus, you can expand your network in as many locations, cities or countries, where your company operates.

In "Rich Dad, Poor Dad", Robert Kiyosaki explains the

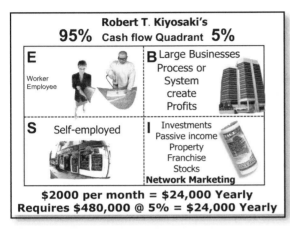

**Robert T. Kiyosaki's**
**95% Cash flow Quadrant 5%**

| E | B Large Businesses |
|---|---|
| Worker Employee | Process or System create Profits |
| S Self-employed | I Investments Passive income Property Franchise Stocks Network Marketing |

**$2000 per month = $24,000 Yearly**
**Requires $480,000 @ 5% = $24,000 Yearly**

Cash Flow Quadrant. It is similar to what you see here. As you can see, most people are on the 95% side. These are the people who are employed by companies for an hourly wage or monthly salary. Also included in the 95% are those people who are self employed operating small businesses where they are working for themselves. On the 5% side is where wealth is built. Only 5% of the people generate income from a <u>system</u>. The desired goal is for you to move from the 95% side to the 5% side where the process or <u>system</u> generates the income or wealth.

Most often, however, the wealth that is generated on the 5% side needs a very sizable start up cash investment. With Network Marketing you can participate in generating wealth through **the "system" of a multi tiered compensation plan** and with a very small start up cash investment. A residual income of $2000 per month is $24,000 in yearly income. In order to make that from an investment, you would need $480,000 to invest at 5% to earn $24,000 yearly. Most people do not have $480,000 to invest. But, your Network Marketing business has the potential to produce this residual income for you and more! So, what is your business worth to you? Only you can answer that question!

# *Chapter 2 - You Say You Want Opportunity?*

 You say you want opportunity. Let me describe it for you. Opportunity is a coin with two faces. On one side is opportunity equal to its face value. On the other side of that same coin are obstacles equal to the face value of the same coin. So, if I have a great opportunity what will be inherent in that great opportunity - a few obstacles - or many? If you're dreaming lofty dreams what must you be prepared to include? There will be many obstacles for you to overcome. There's never been a worthy victory without a struggle.

What does all this mean? The truth is you're not going to accomplish big things <u>without first working on you.</u> You're the one that needs to be worked on. The pursuer of opportunity is you. The better you get, the better your efforts will produce desirable results. Can you see the indisputable connection here? The truth is, and always has been, that you are the one responsible for the outcome. That being said, a truth-revealing question follows: "<u>Are you striving daily for more self-competency?</u>" As you grow, your accomplishments will equally grow. <u>Are you developing your skills</u> or are you like most, simply wishing for things to get better and doing little or nothing to self-improve? If you want to succeed, you must separate your thinking, attitudes, and behavior from the masses of idle dreamers; always "intending" but mostly "pretending."

## *Insight:*

*Each of us has the power of choice and each choice is a step toward some future outcome. There is no escaping this truth. Your life, as it exists today, is a manifestation of your accumulated thoughts, emotions, attitudes, and the choices made by you over time.*

*For example, if learning was unimportant to you, notice the relationship to where you are economically, as a result of that choice. If you complain about your circumstances, or blame others for it, notice the quality of your life as a consequence. If you lack self-motivation, notice the many good things that you and your family will never enjoy. As the great prize fighter, Joe Louis once said, "You can run, but you can not hide." To which I add, "You can avoid the truth, but never its justice." What decisions will you make about your business?*

# *Chapter 3 - Taking Charge*

So, now you're in business. I'll bet you never graduated from a business school or possess an M.B.A. The fact is, most business owners have no formal business education. They all started with an idea, a desire to learn, and mixed both with commitment and work. These are people just like you and me who got tired of the nine-to-five routine, tired of working for someone else, and who decided to go into business for themselves.

One day you make a decision and suddenly you are your own boss. You're the Chairman of the Board, President, Secretary, Shipper, etc. You're the person who is going to make the business succeed or not succeed. Others before you, and just like you, have shown it can be done and in a big way. You can do it too! So let's get going!

**Make a commitment for one year of no turning back effort — you can't quit for at least one year**. Got it? Can't quit! Now, get properly trained — then put your desire and training behind a plan, and success is yours!

The work you will be required to do is not complicated but it must be done often enough to produce the desired result — good income! Ours is a repeat business. We repeat doing simple things well and often, and treat our distributors and retail customers so well that they'll order from us repeatedly.

The products have proved themselves in the marketplace. The compensation plan rewards performance! The only variable

is the person who is selling both. And, that person is you!
　　You can be successful if you take charge.

## Insight:

**　　You will not fail in your business because you lack ability. If you fail it will be because you failed to take responsibility for your own success.**

# *Chapter 4 - But, I am not a salesperson!*

Salesmanship is the most fundamental and natural behavior of the human experience. We've been selling everyday of our lives since birth. No kidding. It's true! You never even got to vote on it. Salesmanship is inextricably tied to your survival instincts. You started in life by selling yourself to your parents, then to your teachers, then to your employers, and also to all the persons you are in relationships with. In fact, if you are having trouble accepting this shocking news, just notice, you are selling again - selling yourself the idea that you are not a salesperson.

Once the mind accepts something as true, i.e., "I am not a salesperson," it immediately looks for stored information, thoughts, and behavior patterns from the past, to support this mental position. You need to be aware that your mind does not always tell you the truth about yourself, nor does it always support your well being in life. In fact, your mind tries to avoid anything that evokes negative emotions and therefore will try constantly, until you catch on, to keep you away from thoughts or activities that position you to experience or confront negatives.

What I want to do is appeal to your experience of "what's so" (how it really works), and not to your thoughts, beliefs, or judgments of "what's so." Your thoughts, beliefs, and judgments are static - they contain your self adopted positions on things and

I maintain many of these positions are stopping you from getting what you want in life.

**Insight:**
**"What's so" is: you've been selling all your life. Why not get better at it and allow selling, that integral function of being alive, to contribute to your personal and financial growth.**

# *Chapter 5 - Customer Objections are O.K.*

**Salesperson's Attitude** Expect objections. They are part of the sales process. Take them in stride. They are not to be viewed as a wall to stop you but simply a small hurdle to overcome.

### Take Objections In Stride

Objections are part of the prospect's defense system. Remember, all prospects, unless they have already made up their minds that they need and want your product before you talk to them, have a learned set of sales-resistant behaviors and attitudes.

You can expect to encounter these behaviors and attitudes in the form of objections throughout your sales career. What to do about them? Learn to include them in your interactions as normal and natural. Don't resist! Include! Objections simply mean they need new information to remove the objection if the objection is valid.

People have various reasons for objections. Some objections can be overcome with more information. Be aware that about 65 percent of the initially expressed objections are not the real ones. In other words, the expressed objection, more often than not, is masking the real objection.

### Handling Objections

Use the tried and proven Feel, Felt, Found technique.

**Salesman:** "I know how you feel. I have plenty of satisfied customers who initially felt that way too and here's what they found." At this point you have neutralized the objection and need to offer more information to your prospect.

**Salesman:** "Let me make a distinction for you." Restate their expressed objection and offer the advantages and benefits of using your product. Follow the same basic procedure for each objection until you see an opening for a trial close.

If the objections offered are vague, you can bet you are dealing with a hidden objection. Hidden objections are usually those that would embarrass the prospect if they were known. An example would be a prospect that simply doesn't have enough money to buy your product or who may be in a relationship where his or her partner has the say about where the money goes.

Here's a suggestion to uncover a hidden objection; pack up your sales materials (prospect's guard is lowered) and say, "Apparently, (Mr. or Ms. Jones), there's some reason why you don't want to buy today, or is there something I failed to tell you? Could you please tell me what it is?" Be quiet here and let the prospect respond. If the real objection comes out, you can deal with it and go for the close. If it is still no go, try for a future appointment.

**Salesman**: "It seems that today is not the best time to be talking to you about this product. I know our product is second to none as it is greatly valued by our thousands of satisfied customers. I'd like to contact you again about this in 30 days, or would 45 days be better, (Mr. or Ms. Jones)?"

If your prospect says no to this, give it up and compliment yourself for not selling out on your commitment to do the best job you are capable of. Move on to the next prospect — one big step closer to a sale. It's all attitude, every bit of it.  **SW, SW, SW Some Will, Some Won't, So What!**

## Back to Objections

If your prospect says, "I'm not interested", simply ask, "Why?" and be silent. After his response you might be able to see a point to focus your next sales attempt around. Remember, most objections that you encounter will fall into one of the following categories:

1. Objection to needing the product.
2. Objection to your product itself.
3. Objection to price.
4. Objection to buying now.
5. Not interested.

Let's take them in order.

**Objection to needing the product.**  Nothing contributes more to the sale of the product as much as creating the value and benefits of the product to the prospect. The entire process of selling can be boiled down to this: "Transferring a conviction from a seller to a buyer." The study time you spend creating value and benefit phrases will pay big dividends.  Preparation, preparation, preparation followed by presentation, presentation, and presentation will produce big dividends.

**Objection to your product itself**.  Be sure to get the prospect's specific objections to your product. What is she comparing it to? Ask direct questions or simply ask, "Why?" If she is comparing your product to another, ask her to tell you the features she likes about the other product and you have an ideal opportunity to illustrate how your product performs that same function in a better way. Simply say, "You've made some excellent points, Ms. Prospect, let me offer some valuable distinctions to shed further light on this."

**Objection to price**. Price objections usually follow the presentation that fails to establish value beyond price. It's really that simple in most cases. Price objections are most often created by the salesman's own attitude about the price of his product. If the salesman deep down has an issue with the price, he will unconsciously create statements and/or body language that in turn create price objections in the prospect.

In effect, the salesman is transmitting price objection stimuli long before it ever shows up in the prospect. If the price is truly greater than your prospect's ability to afford, you have an obligation to move on as pleasantly as possible to the next prospect. If the true objection is price, not affordability, you must counter with values, one after another, to justify the price. When faced with a competitive product with comparable value, stress personal service and your relationship with them, reputation, guarantees, durability, your personal commitment to your prospect, and continued satisfaction with the product. The customer should be told the difference between price and value when handling this object. Remember, "price is what you pay, value is what you get."

**Objection to buying now.** "I'll think it over" is a very common prospect response simply because it works so well on inexperienced sales people. Simply ask, "Ms. Prospect, what information have I failed to give you in order for you to be comfortable with buying this product now?" Wait for the response and don't talk until you get one. Here's where you can use the discount close. "Mr. Prospect, I feel you have seen some real value in this product and I'm going to offer you a special discount of $_.__ if you will place the order now, while I am here.

If that's agreeable to you, we can complete the sales agreement now." Remember that it's your profit margin you're sharing here, so evaluate carefully before using this technique.

**Not interested.** "I'm not interested, thank you" is a catch-all objection usually couched in politeness. To counter this objection, respond with equal politeness.

**Salesman**: "I know how you feel. Most of my customers felt the same way until they found...", and go right into your presentation.

If the prospect insists he is still not interested, take one more stab at it and say, "I don't understand, please excuse me, but what exactly are you not interested in?" State the benefits of your product without pausing for a response until you are through expressing the major features and benefits of your product. If an opening is created, continue on course. If not, move on to the next prospect.

## Closing the Sale

Remember that the purpose of your presentation, demonstration, and all of your sales efforts is to CLOSE THE SALE. Closing a sale is like taking a chance on an opportunity. How many times have you passed up one opportunity for a better opportunity, only to find that the best opportunity was the first one? Don't be afraid to try closing with your prospect before the end of your presentation. It's a way to test the water while you still have an opportunity left to adjust the temperature.

Statistics show that most sales are made after several attempts to close. There is no set of rules to follow on closing. You need to develop awareness about closing signs. They usually show up in the form of questions, casual comments or responses to your questions.

Examples:
- "Is this product guaranteed?"
- "How does your product compare to your competitor's product?" "Is that the only color?"
- "Yes, I agree there's a problem that your product solves."
- "We've been looking at comparable products for some time." "How do I know your product works???"
- "Does your guarantee cover 100% of replacement costs?"
- "Gee, Mildred, what do you think?"----To a third party.

## The Assumption Close

Assume your prospect will buy your product after your presentation. "Well, Mr. Prospect, what we need to do next is fill out this order form. I can accept your personal check or credit card, whichever is more convenient for you? The salesman should always be aware that the only product he can ever sell is a product that offers a solution to one of the prospect's problems or needs.

A successful salesperson is one who develops a total awareness of the countless opportunities each day presents for conversation about his or her products or business opportunity.

If your product benefits all people by design, then all people are your prospects. You need to be willing to engage in conversation that will eventually lead to sharing your product's benefits with another person.

Many times I have used this approach when I am trying to interest the person in my business opportunity. I have made numerous presentations on airplanes, in restaurants, in airports, and at social gatherings by asking one simple question: "What do you do?" No matter what the person responds, I say, "That sounds interesting. Tell me more about it." I am genuinely interested in learning what people like or dislike about their careers and lives. It gives me data to work with when it becomes my turn to talk. The most common response from a person who just finished telling you about what he does is to ask, "And what about you? What do you do?" What a fantastic opportunity — to share my commitment to my product and the benefits it has for my customers, You will discover it's much easier to be heard after you've taken the time to hear someone else's story.

(Although these conversation examples center on product, the subject could just as easily be about your opportunity.)

I make statements like, "I've discovered that most people are really very concerned about their financial futures. Is this a concern that you share as well?" Or I say, "Most people I talk to are very well informed and concerned about this. Have you noticed all the emphasis lately in the news and editorials?" Or I say, "I've been talking to a lot of people and I haven't met a person yet who wasn't aware and concerned. I'd like to share some information with you which I feel confident will support your own awareness and offer you a possible solution."

Sometimes I act perplexed and ask for input from another person (the prospect). Example: "You know John, I'm having a great deal of difficulty dealing with a situation in my business. May I ask you for your insights and suggestions? You see John, I can't understand why everyone I talk to doesn't buy my product. I sell the finest product money can buy. Everybody I talk to has a need for my products. It's priced right. It has great quality. What could I be doing wrong? Here's a brochure that explains the product. See what you think,"

**REMEMBER: You have 2 jobs—selling your products and selling your business opportunity.**

## Rejection — Product or Personal

The biggest single emotion that stops people from sales success is fear of rejection. The people who make it in selling learn to distinguish between product rejection and personal rejection. Those who succeed don't take rejection of product to mean rejection of self. Those who fail at selling almost always view all rejection personally.

***TRUTH: Fear of rejection is one of the most paralyzing fears known to the human experience.***

If you fear rejection, you are already rejected in your own experience of yourself. You'll never get over this crippling, life-draining illusion until you are ready to include rejection as a natural aspect of your life's experience.

To fear rejection is to be run by that fear, which shuts out innumerable positive possibilities for your life. There are literally thousands of experiences you will never have in life if you attempt to avoid rejection. In this process of rejection avoidance you ironically end up with exactly that which you were trying to avoid — rejection. Yes, rejection by the worst critic you know….. you! Let me offer you an insight:

An episode of rejection is an event you can experience, include as part of life and get over. But, to live trying to avoid rejection is a constant psychic attachment to rejection, and you're stuck with it until you confront it and break through to freedom.

**Insight:**

It's okay to be rejected. All people at one time or another experienced rejection. The greatest of men and women have experienced rejection and gone on to accomplish their purpose in life. I can only be stopped by rejection if I am unwilling to include it as okay. After all, it's only my fragile ego that's at stake, and it can always benefit by some humbling. I will take a stand right now and never let fear of rejection stop me again. Refer to **Chapter 21 About Emotions** to understand this concept further.

# Chapter 6 - The Danger Zone -The First 90 Days

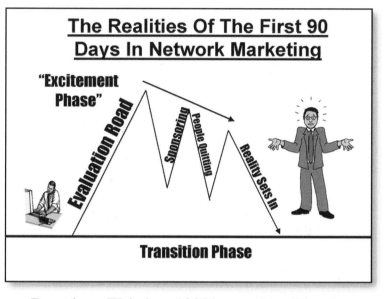

**Premise:  This is a 100% emotional business.**

This is a picture to help you understand the dynamics of the recruiting reality. Once you fully understand what a new representative will go through, you will see the importance of the first 90 days. When people are newly recruited they have the highest excitement level, but they start with the lowest knowledge of the products and understanding of the business. They have the lowest presentation skills, lowest confidence level, and they are the most vulnerable to the negative responses of others. This is the danger zone for the new recruit.  During the first 90 days in the business, they may decide they can't be successful before they know enough and get skilled enough to deserve to succeed.  If you will explain this to your new recruits and help them to make a commitment of one year to get good at their new endeavor, they will have a chance at developing a substantial business and entering into the conviction phase.

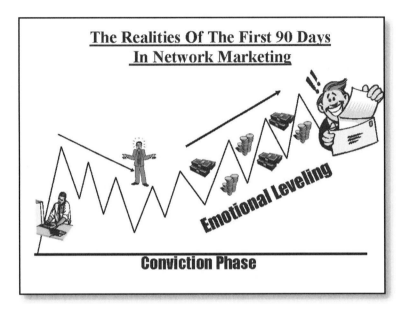

### Insight:

It is once again imperative that the new person make a commitment of one year with no turning back as an option and then keep their word to work their business for one year! They will then enter the conviction phase of their Network Marketing business.

# <u>*Chapter 7 - Recruiting, You Can't Win the Game if You Don't Know How to Play!*</u>

### <u>The reason most people are poor recruiters is because they tell the wrong stories.</u>

First, let me offer you some U.S. background information. According to the Home-Based Business, the Hidden Economy, Home-Based Businesses are a Multi-Billion Dollar a year industry. How? Because of the sheer numbers of people in business for themselves who are now working from home. The extremely low start up costs, flexible hours, and the internet are fueling the growth of the home based business segment. Today there are hundreds of thousands of people who enjoy the freedom and benefits of owning their own home-based businesses. The home based business sector is growing in importance and diversity and offers opportunities for entrepreneurs and at home professionals in every demographic and ethnic group.

Do you know the major reasons why people are flocking to Home-Based Businesses?

1. They are tired of the commute to work and the high cost of gas.
2. They are tired of the stress associated with dealing with their boss.
3. They are tired of the pressures of their job demands and the anxiety about keeping them are very draining on their mental attitudes.
4. Their lack of job satisfaction.
5. They get little or no recognition or appreciation.

6. They desire more quality time for family and leisure activity.
7. They finally recognize that financial freedom will never be provided by their jobs.
8. They experience high levels of dissatisfaction and frustration about where they are in life.
9. They are tired of ongoing accumulation of personal debt.
10. They have come to the point where they feel they must change the direction of their careers and bet on themselves.
11. They are attracted to the low financial investment needed to start-up and operate an in-home business.
12. They have a recognized need to experience new excitement and hope for a better future.
13. They are fed up with needing two incomes to survive.
14. They see the clock moving forward while their standard of living stands still or goes backward.
15. They become educated about the legal tax deductions available to the SERIOUS home-based business entrepreneurs. (Check on these with your tax expert)

What happens to these "serious" home entrepreneurs over time?  Well, according to Office Computing Magazine's Survey in the United States:

- 96% do not plan on going back to the Rat Race.
- 65% are realizing their financial dreams.
- 70% said "getting new business" is one of their 5 greatest challenges.
- **61% said they would be more successful if they got focused and better organized.**

Author, Al Siebert in his book, "Survivor Personality"

said, "People have to become more self-reliant and flexible, more resilient than ever in modern history".

All of these conditions make for a very fertile recruiting environment. However, as a recruiter it will do you little good to know all the wonderful facts about your company, its products and management, or its compensation plan, if you don't address first what people are looking for to improve in their lives. If you don't identify the situation that they are trying to leave behind or improve, how can you expect to get their sincere attention to your opportunity?

People listen first for possible solutions to **their concerns and problems** long before they will hear anything else you are saying. If you put the cart before the horse, it will be very difficult to travel very fast or very far. You need to identify first with your prospect's circumstances by telling a story which connects with their personal situation.

Your story should "set the stage" for serious listening to the opportunity's specifics which follow the story. Let me explain it this way, a person could be sick with a deadly disease and not be consciously aware of that disease until pain occurs. Once pain is felt however, it is very easy to talk about relief, needed treatment and eventual cure.

Notice that the surfaced pain got their undivided attention! It's the same with recruiting. Unless your opening story addresses what's going on with most people's lives today, you will find it very difficult to open their minds to your opportunity. They won't listen to a possible cure for a disease that no one has brought to their attention.

## The best recruiters are those individuals who do the following:

1. They are excellent storytellers.
2. The stories they tell relate to the people they are telling them to.
3. They exhibit total confidence in their voice, eyes, gestures and what they are communicating.
4. They do not pressure.
5. They prepare well and do not "wing it".
6. They know that if they keep on presenting to new prospects they are guaranteed two certain results which are a) they will become better presenters and b) they will find the people who want what they are presenting, their network marketing opportunity.
7. They professionally inform their prospects.

Finally, you must remember these two essential principles if you are to be a good recruiter:

1. **Tentative is NO POWER! If you are still wondering if your business will work for you, you cannot become a good recruiter.**
2. **All of selling (and we are selling) is reduced to a personal conviction being passed from you, the seller, to a prospective buyer.**

Now, what stands out most about these insights? Well, here's what I see, the words "Serious Entrepreneur" are something to ponder as it relates to your own efforts to build your business.  <u>And, what about success being related to better focus and organized effort?</u>     How do you measure up?  What about your confidence level in yourself and your opportunity?  Is it now always being reflected in the tone, power and content of your words?

You need to square up with the reasons others can successfully recruit while you can't seem to.  Could it be as simple as; their number of presentations, invitations, one-on-ones, and 3-way calls greatly exceed yours?  You see, it is not really so difficult to become a great recruiter after all.  All you need to do is get your initial stories on target, and then present them with vigor, confidence, and in the right order and right frequency to get the results you are after.

**Lastly, tell those stories to the people who desire to become successful.  So, keep on getting better at presenting to more people and you will one day find yourself in the Circle of Network Marketing Champions!**

<u>**Insight:**</u>
**The best recruiters are good at transferring their convictions and confidence from themselves to their prospects.**

# *Chapter 8 -Prospecting and Recruiting*

So, who are you going to approach about your new business? Your friends, acquaintances and family members are the best places to start. Remember, this is **relationship marketing.** Everyone gets started by making a list of people they know. It's a very good idea to keep yourself organized by making a list of persons you are going to talk to and then keeping separate pages for each one. I like to keep a notebook that is solely for notes on prospects. At the beginning of the notebook, I outline the information that I tell everyone on my list.

I make a list of all the benefits of owning your own business, knowing that most people start on a part time basis until they have built their income to a level to justify going full time. Then, I give a brief overview of the company, and its history of commitment to quality products. I emphasize the training and support that is available.

Be sure to mention the following:

- Joining a Solid Company
- Solid Support
- Flexible Hours
- Being Your Own Boss
- Quality Training Provided
- Exciting Travel
- Increased Freedom
- Unlimited Income Potential

• Legal Tax Advantages of Business Ownership
• A Proven Business Concept
• Ability to Pass Business to children

Then you ask which of these benefits interests them the most.  You wait for the response.  You must listen to know what motivates the person to be interested in your business opportunity.  Is it more family time?  Is it more money for a child's education?  Is it being their own boss?  Is it fun and new friends?

You must write these things down on a page designated for each prospect, so you remember what motivates the individual you are trying to recruit.

**Remember, recruiting is a process.**  Always be prepared to leave behind good company materials, magazines, DVD's. brochures, etc.   Dream stealers will be there after you get a person excited and these company materials help to keep your prospect from getting discouraged.  You must follow up with personal visits and phone calls.  If your prospect says yes to the business, it is very important to start training that person within 24 hours.  Plan a follow-up at the time they join.

Here are some suggestions on ways to approach your friends:

1. "Mary, lets get together this afternoon for a cup of coffee.  There is something I would like to talk to you

about."
2.  "Mary, how would you like to have _____?" Mention a benefit you think would get Mary excited. "I'm going to come over this afternoon and tell you about it."
3.  "Mary, you may not be interested in what I am about to offer you, but I simply could not resist telling you anyway. Can I stop by for a few minutes today?"
4.  "Mary, are there some things you'd buy for yourself or your family right now if you had the money? (Listen for response) Great! I'm going to show you something really exciting. Can I meet with you for a few minutes today?"
5.  "Mary, do you keep your business options open? I have been investigating a new way to earn income. When would be a good time to get together?"

You can now create several more approaches on your own. The key is being brief. Be positive. Ask for the appointment. Bring excellent materials to leave behind. Don't explain the details on the phone unless you are long distance sponsoring. Be sincere, enthusiastic, and honest! **Your job is to sell them on their dreams and goals and guide them to their destination!**

## Remember, when the prospect is listening to the opportunity, they are listening for only 3 things.

1.  **Can I trust this person telling the story and the story itself?**
2.  **Is this for me?**
3.  **Can I see myself successful if I join?**

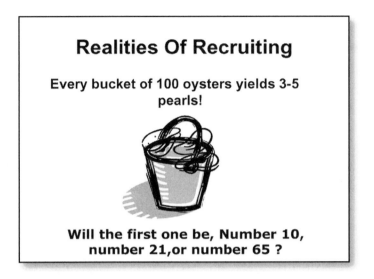

**Realities Of Recruiting**

Every bucket of 100 oysters yields 3-5 pearls!

Will the first one be, Number 10, number 21,or number 65 ?

## Insight:

You want to think of recruiting as shucking oysters as this graphic depicts. There will always be 3 out of 100 oysters that have a pearl. But, you don't know which will contain the pearl. So it is with your recruiting efforts. Don't get discouraged when the first three people do not join you in your network marketing business. If you present to 100 people, over time you will sponsor a number of representatives. However, only three to five will become Big Business Building Stars in your downline. It's the numbers! You just don't know where the five are until they declare themselves and perform.

## *Chapter 9 - Finding Business Partners*

**Remember: Your primary job is to provide enough factual information to stimulate interest.**

**When you find a person's reason for doing, you have found the key to his will.**

When your new representative's attention is focused on what he plans to buy with the money he will make, his emotions will play powerfully on his will to endure. Money in itself is only a symbol. It can symbolize power, success, independence, romance, freedom, security, smartness, indifference to society's demands for conformity, and many other things all different, and each more or less important to each individual.

The illusion that people work for money is still strong, but motivationally inaccurate. **People work for what money's power represents in terms of things they can possess, control, experience, or give to others.** The instinct to possess money is tied directly to what one imagines himself doing once he has it. We humans have a very strong instinct to possess, to call things "mine". This is why I like to encourage the use of Goal Boards that have colorful pictures of the objects one desires. Pictures will communicate desired thoughts more profoundly than the most eloquent words. They also serve as a constant reminder of your "why" for doing the business.

Young business building recruits dream of going to new exciting places, of travelling to romantic settings, of driving exciting cars, meeting exciting people, and enjoying new thrills and adventures in life.

Older prospective business partners enjoy some of the same things that the young do, but they are not their primary source of motivation. The older person is more security conscious, interested in what can happen for them if they commit - what benefits are available to their families if they get involved. The older person is trying to gain security for his or her old age, for a "rainy day." In general, as people grow older the fear or caution motive becomes stronger. They need more time to evaluate and will generally make commitment decisions in a 2 or 3 step processes.

Whether young or old, all people respond to being accepted as they are and appreciated for what they do. In your presentations, use words and pictures that appeal to the part of the mind that visualizes. This method arouses attention because we humans think in pictures. Mental pictures arouse emotions, so illustrate, demonstrate, and dramatize your story. Show people they can get what they want out of your opportunity and they will join your network.

### Insight:
**You can lead a horse to a watering hole, but he may not drink. Therefore, look for thirsty horses! Don't prejudge who you think will or will not be successful. You will discover who is successful by what they do, not what they say they will do!**

# *Chapter 10 - Traits of a Good Sponsor*

**Network Marketing**

*"People Helping People!"*

In the back of this manual, you are going to rate yourself on specific leadership skills and then work to improve them. If you are going to succeed in Network Marketing you will need to be a good coach. Coaching involves helping your group succeed. This is why Network Marketing works so well. It is truly "People Helping People. The more your group members prosper, the more you prosper. This is the essence of a successful Network Marketing business.

When I sponsor a new person I ask this question. "Do I have permission for the next 90 days to be your personal coach?" If they say yes, then you ask them," What about their past coaches did they like best and also what did they not like?" This will tell you much about how to coach this person. It will also allow you to help the new recruit going forward as he or she faces the many pitfalls of the first 90 days.

Here are some of the coaching skills that will help you to be a big support to your team members:

- Knowledgeable
- Patient
- Consistent
- Keen Observer
- Excellent Listener
- Trustworthy
- Firm, But Caring Demeanor
- Direct Communicator

- Sets Performance Expectations
- Stimulate Action
- Demand Accountability
- Positive thinker
- Integrity
- Intense desire to achieve
- Charisma
- Persistent
- Courage

## Here are 10 things that a good leader avoids:

- Avoid "The Big Ego" syndrome – Having to be the Biggest Dog Attitude
- Avoid egocentric emphasis in your language
- Avoid thinking you have accomplished your business alone
- Avoid thinking your title places you as superior to others in your group.
- Avoid being "bossy" with others in your group
- Avoid thinking you know more than other developing leaders in your group
- Avoid having to be the center of attention and always shining the spotlight on yourself.
- Avoid needing Stage Domination
- Avoid being enrolled in negative conversations with their downline members
- Avoid losing belief and focus when having to deal with business problems or change.

## Here are four essential Elements to your MLM Success:

1. **A Red Hot Desire To Succeed**
2. **Humility To Be Coached**
3. **An Unwavering Commitment to necessary actions**
4. **Persistence**

## This is failure in Network Marketing:

- Poor preparation – no definite activity plan
- Lack of practice and steady improvement of inviting and presenting skills.
- A small or non-existant contact list.
- Irregular involvement at weekly meetings, leadership, information, and inspiration calls.
- Seldom use upline expert for 3 way recruiting calls.
- Has a "once in a while" inconsistent work ethic.
- Never attend a company convention.
- Strong tendency to look at the negatives to take the focus away from their own lack of performance.
- Lack passion and commitment to reach the top.

## Listening- The Skill To Master For Super Star Team Building

1. <u>Remember, you have 2 ears and 1 mouth!</u>
2. Don't miss a single word coming from your prospect.
3. Lean slightly toward the person you are listening to.
4. Maintain attentive eye contact.
5. Ask questions when appropriate.
6. Don't interrupt.
7. End with a sincere expression of appreciation for their time and attention.
8. Be mindful that listening is the most important skill in effective coaching.

<u>**Insight:**</u>

**When you are talking, you are providing information. But, when you are listening, you are gaining far more important information!**

# *Chapter 11 - It's Now or Never!*

Perhaps now is the perfect time to take stock of the true status of our financial assets and liabilities, and then examine to what extent we are truthfully pursuing our common business, **our network marketing opportunity.** Let's do it now!

Many of us declare that we want freedom from economic stress, while at the same time spending most of our potentially productive hours, worrying about our economic state, rather than working with a sustained and serious effort for a remedy. There is a strong tendency for us to tilt toward excuses for our lack of financial health, rather than look squarely at the truth of our condition and the real causes. They are …. "a lack of clearly defined goals"; "an opportunity we are enrolled in but not passionately engaged in"; "an over-reaction to the negative actions and opinions of others"; "the inability to stay disciplined with the work required." All of this and more serve to make certain our financial dreams stagnate or yet worse, die.

Personal financial health and vitality come to those who seize opportunity and not dabble with it. It comes to those who include what I call **"impeding obstacles"** that are sure to be plentiful along the road to success. These include the frustrations of putting time and sincere effort into assisting team members who say they want success, but act quite to the contrary. For example, the countless people you invite to meetings who say yes, but don't show; the reps who stay on but do not move up; the occasional corporate misfires, mistakes, and unclear policies, including the lost paper work, the occasional billing errors; the feeling at times that no one of authority is responding or even listening to our concerns, and the list goes on.

**LET'S GET REAL!** Do you really think it is any different anyplace else? The truth is there is no shortage of this "impeding obstacle list' any place where there are people, human beings, collected together  under any business, educational, or governmental enterprise. It's just part of all business and administrative enterprises anywhere. It just so happens that some organizations are better than others at keeping it from the masses. However, in our business, most of what bothers us is pretty much in our face. Thus it is easier for us to react with frustration, sometimes anger, lethargic business actions, or just plain stagnation and inaction. All of these reactions, although on the surface seem justified, are totally counter-productive to your personal success. They serve only to alter your attitude, dampen your enthusiasm, weaken your belief, and throttle your initiative to work your business. Unfortunately, the company's misfires combine with your negative reactions and the only result will be defeat for you! Don't let that happen to you! Why? Because your company will go on and eventually either eliminate totally or greatly improve most of their "impeding obstacles". Why? Because they have millions of dollars at stake combined with a firm commitment and true passion for getting their side of the business equation right so that all involved will win. In addition, the company owners and corporate leaders really do care. They possess the desire, the character, the will, the integrity, and work ethics to lead you to victory. So what are we, the independent representatives, left with to decide? It really comes down to a simple choice between belief and non-belief in your personal eventual victory.

 A good company will win, and I firmly believe it will. And, if you personally did not stay the course with full vigor and commitment, and you leave or simply stop, the only loser will be you! **<u>Maturity in the business world includes a great deal of tolerance for things that need to be improved, but must be endured until they are improved.</u>**

If you are ever to reach your goal of financial freedom, you will need to first be realistic about your expectations of others, be it the company or your reps. Second, you will need to develop mastery of emotional response when things, events, or people don't fit your personal wishes, preferences, or pictures of how you think things should be.

"Circumstances", and "people" will always be as they are until they change and not one second before. So, if you aspire to be a success in the months and years ahead, you will need to dig in your own heels, adjust your mental attitudes, and act as though it were impossible to fail. And, I'm betting that if you can do this, you won't fail.

**Insight:**

In Success magazine, Charles King, PhD. in business, Harvard University, Marketing Professor, University of Illinois and expert on Network Marketing said, "During the 3-5 years of hard work it takes to build a substantial downline, you'll be equity driven. However, once your downline is in place, your investment becomes a cash machine."

# *Chapter 12 - Meetings*

**Eighty percent of your effectiveness depends upon your own belief and attitude. The remaining twenty percent is based upon content.**

## Present Yourself As A Professional

- <u>Consider your appearance</u> – Your Prospects will!
- <u>Consider how you speak</u> – Voice tonality and clarity
- <u>Consider your poise</u> – What aura or demeanor emanates from you that conveys your power, caring, self assurance, and sincerity – Do you inspire confidence and promote a relaxed atmosphere?
- <u>Dependability</u> – Do you keep your word?
- <u>Honesty</u> – Are you grounded in a solid commitment to operate from integrity? Does your audience feel it?
- <u>Integrity</u> is "An uncompromising adherence to a code of moral, artistic, or other values." Do your words convey this quality?
- <u>Initiative-Resourcefulness</u> –Are they part of you?
- <u>Confidence</u> – If you believe in yourself, others will be more likely to believe in you. It is built on the foundation of adequacy, which only comes from study and application. Do you demonstrate total confidence as you present?
- <u>Enthusiasm</u> – The priceless ingredient that pays the biggest dividends in sales. You stimulate others

to act when you possess an enlivened spirit. Is your enthusiasm real or fake?

- <u>Perseverance</u> – Remember the human will is better drawn than it is pushed. Your purpose needs to be big enough to carry you through the dry seasons of labor, frustration, and fatigue.

## In-Home Meetings

Greet people enthusiastically. Begin with introductions. Keep the mood exciting! Serve only snacks and soft drinks, no alcoholic beverages.

Encourage anyone who has something exciting to share to do so. Have they received a large bonus check? Won a trip? Helped a friend? Let them share, but keep this process brief. (One or two minutes maximum)

Personalize the meeting by stating your reasons for being excited about your business. State your personal commitment to provide service, training, and leadership to anyone who joins.

## Give an enthusiastic summary of all the strengths of your company.

1. We are strong financially.
2. We are leaders in our products or services.
3. We have an impeccable history of company integrity.
4. We sell the greatest products or services available anywhere.
5. Our income opportunity is unequaled.

6. We are committed to excellence.

The body of your meeting may be (a) product and (b) the business opportunity. Work out the presentations you feel most comfortable with. The key to success is to be yourself, be properly prepared, and present with confidence and enthusiasm.

Have your product props set up prior to the meeting. Your office and product display should be neat. Clutter scares people and stimulates a negative thought flow.

Do not try to talk about all of the products. Select a few and be brief in your explanations about each. Sell the customer the benefits of the product, i.e., "Your skin will feel and look younger "You'll be amazed at your increased energy level"... "I'm excited about the excellent results my customers report back to me"," People love our services!", "My customers send me lots of referrals!" etc.

### Insight:
**At all meetings your primary objective is to SELL, not entertain! Do not wander. Stay with a program outline. Start on time. End on time!**

# *Chapter 13 - Telephone*

You make your first impression solely by voice on the phone. Therefore, smile when you speak and the smile will project as a friendly soft tone. Research has indicated that standing while talking on the phone increases your communicating energy. The rewards of telephone prospecting go to those who have thoroughly prepared themselves and are able to work from a well-organized plan of action, instead of relying on hit-and-miss methods.

## Some Ideas About Telephone Work

1. Draw up a list of prospects.
2. Develop a sales script of working notes.
3. Prepare answers for the most common objections for your script.
4. Organize your work area for comfort and efficiency.
5. Determine the best hours of the day or evening to call your prospects.
6. Have your date book handy.
7. Plan some opening remarks (script).
8. Know the buyer and not just the product.
9. Offer solutions to objections (script).
10. Be prepared to close the sale or appointment.

A good telephone presentation consists of carefully selected words and must appeal to the ear, and the imagination of the listener.

### The Three way call

This is a tried and proven tool to aid in the recruiting process. When you tell a prospect that you would like them to talk to your upline expert it is very important to "edify your expert."

1. Relate how successful your upline is and tell something about their backround and values.
2. Identify your expert as extremely knowledgeable.
3. Let your prospect know what a nice, non pushy person he or she will be speaking with.
4. Introduce your prospect to your upline expert and let the expert do all the talking unless you are asked for your input.
5. Remember that stories sell better than data, so use testimonials and success stories.
6. End your 3 way by asking your prospect a simple question;

***Do you see any reason why this business would not be of benefit to you at some level?*** There are only three answers to this question.

### People fall into 3 categories.

1. They are not interested. Ask politely why and move on.
2. Those that have more questions and considerations! Work diligently and quickly with these.
3. Those that are ready and want to get involved and begin..

## Insight:

**Find a partner to practice your presentation with until you are confident and comfortable.**

# *Chapter 14 - The Cycle of Success*

**Appointments are the first step toward success in your business.**

Here are some questions you could ask to help you get the appointment:

1. Would you listen to an exciting opportunity?
2. Do you have a need for additional income?
3. 1 found a way to make some excellent income by working with people. Would you be interested in hearing about it?
4. Have you ever considered having your own business?
5. Do you know any people who would be interested in a part- time career that offers excitement and income potential?
6. If you could earn extra money this year with a part-time business, could you get excited?
7. Would you be interested in increasing your present income substantially?
8. I have found an opportunity that offers me the kind of future I've always dreamed of. Could I talk to you about it?

Note: Do not try to explain anything about the business when you are setting up the appointment. The purpose of the meeting is to explain the business. The purpose of the telephone call is to set up the appointment.

**Duplication of effort equals multiplication of income! How many people you sponsor is not nearly as important as how many become leaders.**

The smart business builders may sponsor many but work closely with a few — those who are serious and want to become successful. Using this method, you build a large Personal Group Volume while at the same time develop independent legs, building your residual income.

**SPONSORING is the key to building a large income in your business.**

## The Meeting or One-on-One Presentation

When setting the appointment, ask for only 30 minutes, and then set the date and time.

- Don't be late.
- Do be neat and dress appropriately for the situation.
- Don't be flashy or sloppy.
- Do be prepared to discuss the benefits.
- Don't waste time on small talk.
- Do stay within your requested 30 minutes.
- Don't forget to observe and listen.
- Do start your presentation 3 to 5 minutes after you arrive.
- Don't leave the appointment without trying to sell or sponsor.
- Do ask for the result you want.
- Don't get discouraged

**There are really only 12 Steps to Success in your Network Marketing business.**

1.  Learn about your company. Love all the products. Believe in both.
2.  Set some very specific Goals and outline Activity Schedules to support your written goals.
3.  Work your business 15 to 20 hours each week.
4.  Have 3 sponsoring appointments each week, never less.
5.  Hold a weekly meeting in your home and one in someone else's home.
6.  Train and motivate your group.
7.  Have adequate promotional inventory to supply your group.
8.  Take responsibility for maintaining your own positive mental attitude.
9.  Be willing to lead by example.
10. Do what is expected of all great leaders, keep on in the face of adversity,
11. Be honest in all of your business dealings.
12. Love yourself, your representatives, and your business.

**Insight:**

**Leaders keep sponsoring because they understand the principle and power of multiplication. Leaders teach their distributors this principle and then encourage them to expand their own understanding and expectations of the possibilities that can result from this understanding.**

# Section 2
## Some Important Psychological Insights

# *Chapter 15 - Understanding Reality Filters*

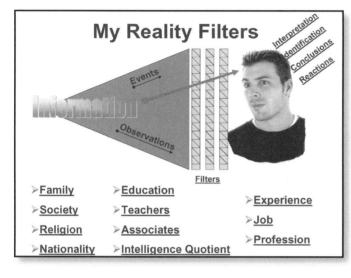

This is how we all create our own personal realities. To change our conditions in life, we might need to change or abandon some of the filters we have fixed in our minds and replace them with new ones. What are the filters that we each view our reality through? That all depends on who you are and what have been your influences. So, when we hear about a new idea, we all hear it differently, through our own reality filters. Those filters include your race, religion, family, education, nationality, IQ, profession and so on. We are constantly processing information in our minds through the filters of what we already know. This is why no two people hear about an opportunity exactly the same. Knowing this should make you more relaxed in the recruiting process. People decide through their filters, not yours. So, relax and just get good at presenting your products and opportunity and realize some will be interested and some will not. What you do have control over is how you react to your prospects decision to get involved or not get involved. Keep your emotions under control. The more you eliminate the emotional highs and the lows during the recruiting of individuals, the better your chances of staying in the business long enough to sponsor good strong team members.  Keep a mental picture of the emotional response of a waitress in a restaurant serving coffee.  She does not get excited when someone would like more coffee and she does not get depressed because someone does not want coffee.  So, when you are in the process of recruiting individuals, tell yourself that, "Some will, some won't, so what!"


**Insight:**
    **"Change is the result of changing the FILTERS!"**

# *Chapter 16 - How We Create Our Personal Reality*

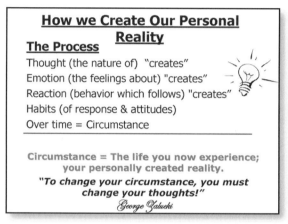

**How we Create Our Personal Reality**

**The Process**

Thought (the nature of) "creates"
Emotion (the feelings about) "creates"
Reaction (behavior which follows) "creates"
Habits (of response & attitudes)
Over time = Circumstance

Circumstance = The life you now experience;
your personally created reality.

*"To change your circumstance, you must change your thoughts!"*
*George Zalucki*

Our thoughts create our emotions, which creates our reactions, which creates our habits, which over time creates our circumstances in life. They are all tied together. So, to change our circumstances in life, we must change our thoughts!! We are creating our personal reality or the life we now experience one thought at a time. If we think something is too hard we will find the proof that it is and therefore, our project is over before we start. It is our thoughts about things that literally create our experiences in life.

**Example: Two men sat behind prison bars, one saw mud the other one saw stars!!** The two men had the exact same circumstances, but they chose different thoughts about their circumstances and therefore had totally different experiences of the exact same event.

We need to engage our power of thought and subconscious by imagination and visualization. All of us know this power. We just don't all tap into it. Most of us have had the experience of needing to be up at an early hour for a very important reason. We were so concerned that we might not awaken that we set 3 alarm clocks. Then, one minute before the alarm, we woke up and turned all the alarm clocks off. Who was keeping time for you? You made such a firm command to yourself that you could not miss awaking that your subconscious kept time for you while you were sleeping!!! This is the awesome power of thought.

**Insight:**
   **If you think you can or you can  not, you will prove yourself right!**

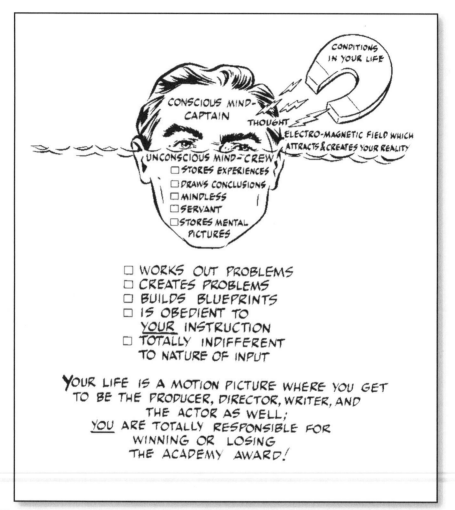

### Insight:

**We all create our own destiny by the thoughts of our minds. We can, therefore, create a new and better destiny by better thinking which will lead to better choices, and thereby create better results.**

# *Chapter 17 - Thought and Destiny*

**If you expect to achieve results in business that you never in your past accomplished, then you must expect to employ yourself at a level never before attempted.**

People keep looking for the secret of success. The secret lies in the mirror! Success today, yesterday or tomorrow will always be the result of hard work, learning from our mistakes and failures, loyalty to your company and your business associates, integrity in all your dealings, plus unrelenting effort until you arrive at your determined goal. Now, if the mirror says back to you….. "That's who you are!" Then success is sure to come your way. But, if not,  then whatever is lacking must be developed and added to you. In a nutshell, your thoughts, methods of business, and your actions must be improved or changed. Remember, before you can harvest you must plant, cultivate, and nurture.

Before you even begin to pursue your objectives, you need to vividly picture yourself achieving your goals. To be successful you must fill your mind with a continuous flow of success-orientated thoughts. **Always remember this undisputable truth. The unsuccessful non-achieving person has feasted on a mental diet devoid of authentic goals, hope, faith and self-belief. Conversely the successful, achieving person has feasted on a mental diet laden with specific intent, hope, faith, and self-belief.**

Science has taught us that the universe has a very powerful force called "electro –magnetism." When it comes to the human mind there is the law of attraction. Postive human behavior, unlike in physics, draws positive, and negative human behavior draws negative. Therefore, what you hold resolutely in your mind, as a desired end must come to pass if your vision is matched with sustained effort; and to sustain effort you need faith and self-belief. Until the individual accepts and utilizes his own power to shape his own life, he can expect little more than a life of survival or mediocrity at best.

Our thoughts are contagious! They can only attract and then duplicate themselves in like kind. We all magnetize the conditions in our lives in accordance with the nature of our own individual thoughts. Examine your present life as it now exists, and you will see with honest reflection that your thoughts, behaviors, and choices have been the creative force of the life you now live.

"To change the conditions of my life, I need to change the thoughts of my mind!" Nothing else will do it! Every action I take is directed by the thoughts I engage in prior to the action I take. When I am happy, it is my thoughts about the experience that makes me happy. And, so it is when I am sad. It is my thoughts about the condition which saddens me that creates my sadness. Before I can give up on something or someone, I must engage in thoughts about giving up. When I persevere through tough times or circumstances, it is my thoughts of persevering that keep me going.

Your thoughts will carry you through all obstacles and setbacks if they are of a nature to do so. Your unshakable conviction that you will eventually succeed can only be created and sustained by the nature and content of the thoughts from your own mind as you pursue your goal. You must shift your thoughts from uncertainty to certainty; from indecisiveness to decisiveness; from doubt to faith; from inaction to action. You can expect tremendous dividends if you rid your mind of negative thoughts which in turn trigger negative emotions and attitudes. **A word of caution- do not dismiss this information if you truly want to succeed.**

Remember, the scoffer, the skeptic, or the unbeliever can never light the fire from within that is needed to succeed. The scoffer or the skeptic will always avoid the intensity of clear purpose because he knows to engage in the contest will only reveal his true character and underdeveloped abilities. As for the unbelievers, they have lost the capacity to see good things happening for themselves. They don't much enjoy the condition of their lives and being stuck in a negative mindset. They are fearful of the future or simply avoid thinking about it. All these unbelievers have lost the capacity to risk victory or defeat and, in so doing, spend their lives in the house of survival where dreams don't live.

If we are to achieve our desired goals we must make a powerful resolve to change the pictures of our mind. Yes, those negative pictures that have limited your accomplishments to date.

It is only you who can decide. No more backward looks. Only forward visions supported by the courage to persist, a passion for action, and a sustaining faith that you can and will overcome or endure whatever you encounter along the way will be accepted.

We all know someone who has dramatically changed. We

were awestruck as to what really happened to them.  **Their lives were changed in accordance and agreement with the nature of their new thoughts.**

Let me explain.  Old thoughts and bad habits were not changed by "will power."  No they were changed by new thoughts that then began the process of developing new habits.  Those new thoughts were the genesis and sustaining source of what you observed as change.  Regardless of the nature of the change, be it good or bad, the process is exactly the same.  **The change was caused by the nature and content of "thoughts."  These new thoughts, then created new attitudes, behaviors, habits, and results.**

"As you think, so shall you become," is not simply a religious cliché!  No, it is a law of human behavior and as such it is the creative force of your personal attitudes and behaviors, and therefore over time is the creative force of the circumstances we find in our present lives.

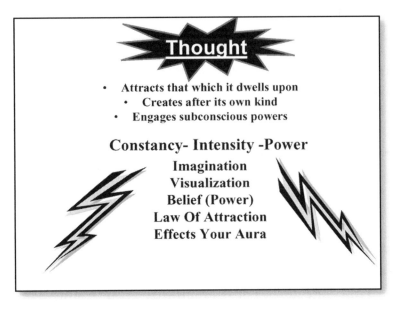

## *Dynamic Energy Results*

**Insight:**

Every choice has a consequence or outcome; and every choice was preceded by a thought of what to choose. Therefore, choose your thoughts with great care because they are directing the entire course of your life!

# *Chapter 18 - How To Achieve Your Intentions*

When you dream lofty dreams, be prepared for obstacles because your mind will convince you that many things stand in your way. If your mind says, "This goal is going to be tough to achieve," you will walk through this world looking for evidence of your thought. And, whenever evidence shows up, you will say, "See I told you this goal is too tough."

## A Necessary Understanding

A goal has two sides. On one side is what you want. On the other side is what you don't want to do to achieve it. The only sure way to overcome obstacles and achieve your goal is to surrender to your purpose. Declare what it is you want and claim it as your birthright! You must have established clear and precise goals that you passionately want to achieve.

That done, the success or failure of your goal will ultimately be determined by dozens of small decisions you make everyday. With each decision, ask your self just two simple questions.

- **Question #1:** "Is what I'm about to do now going to lead me toward my goal?" If you answer "no" and if you are truthful with yourself, you will begin to change and direct your behavior toward your goals. (You will be surprised to see how many times your present behavior is not aligned with your goals.)
- **Question #2:** "Is the decision I am about to make going to harm another human being?" If the answer is no, proceed with full vigor! If the answer is yes, rethink and develop a new course of action.

Too often we rationalize our attitudes and behaviors that are inconsistent with attaining our goals, not realizing the eventual consequence of such folly. We rationalize that we don't have enough time. We tell ourselves that everyone's doing it this way, or it's not such a big deal. Compound this over many decisions and a little compromise soon becomes a lot of compromise. Pretty soon you find yourself completely off course.

Let's face it! The accumulated decisions we make..... make us! That's right! The consequence of our choices makes us what we are. We have all made bad choices in our lives, and to varying degrees, we have all stopped growing and have become reactors to life instead of creators of life. To begin correcting it, we must first acknowledge these facts, accept the truth, and then resolve to be committed to doing it another way. **Commitment to personal growth is what transforms an ordinary person into something extraordinary.**

## The Real Object of Growth Is You!

Your world "outside" of you will prove over time to have been created by the world "inside" of you. You can't do great things without working on you. The better you get, the closer you will get to your objective. **It is all about personal commitment to personal growth and personal responsibility for your results.**

Commitment is doing the thing you said you would do long after the mood you said it in has left you. Think about that for a moment. Commitment is doing whatever it takes, for as long as it takes. Most of us are committed until...until it is too tough, until it doesn't fit our schedule, until we have something else to do. Our minds bombard us with an endless list of "untils."

Surrendering to your objective includes disciplining your mind to stay with the commitment. Take a stand! **Persistence creates the wings upon which the glory of victory rides in all areas of life.** Persistence shows clear dynamic evidence of your faith in yourself and your objectives. **Commitment plus**

**persistence transforms a promise into a reality.** And, the kind of persistence that leads to victory is always tied to surrender to purpose.

Finally, you will accomplish your goals for one reason, and one reason only; because **YOU** said **YOU** would. All other reasons fail you sooner than later   **So, become your word**. Do what you speak with clear intentions. Commit to it and tie into the power of persistence. And, eventually, victory is yours! You can bet on it!

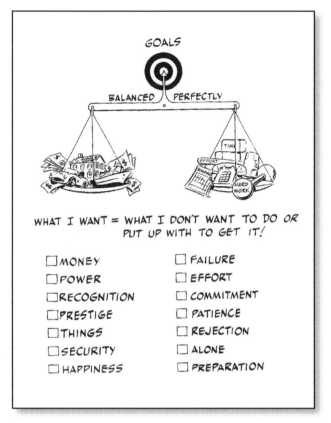

## Insight:

      **These two will always be in balance. The more I want, the more I must endure what I do not want to include. An unfortunate observation—most people would rather endure the hardships associated with having little money than the hardships associated with having lots of money. To the mind, they require the same energy. Once again, the balance is perfect. What people want is on one side and what they do not want to do or put up with is on the other. We can show people our business and tell them the simplicity of it, but they do need to understand what they are facing. If they can include this reality, they can expect eventual success!**

# *Chapter 19 - Without Failure There Can Be No Success!*

"The superhighway to success is laden with disappointments, frustrations, and countless failures." It is how you handle these realities that make all the difference in the outcome of your life and business. The key is "inclusion" and **"stick ability"!** No one who ever achieved a big goal avoided these three "wreckers" of success. This trio overtakes the weak, but "steels" the strong with greater determination. If you can't avoid them, and you seriously desire to win, then you must get tough and include them. They will eventually become less burdensome, but they will never completely disappear. That is just the way it is! Remember, there is no traffic jam at the top. You need to be resilient to get there.

**General George Patton said, "I don't measure a man's success by how high he climbs, but by how high he bounces back when he hits obstacles."**

There may be many roads to Rome but there is only a very narrow road that leads to financial success; but it is very well defined. A person committed to reaching financial independence will get on that road and not detour one bit. The success road is very well lit, with lots of caution signs, and you can be certain that potholes and bumps will be encountered along the way. But, you can also be assured that if you stay on it you will eventually succeed.

If winning is about a firmly rooted desire to succeed, then one must get their mind in focus, and their emotions under control. Otherwise expect to lose. A clear vision of "What" you want, and "Why" you want it, is the starting point, and also the "magnet" that draws your will into action.

Remember that the human will is very reluctant to be pushed, but it is easily drawn toward a vividly desired goal. You can make your goals inevitable by employing a vivid and sustaining picture of what you are striving for; be it a new car, a new home, a new career, a new lifestyle, or financial independence. Henry Thoreau said, **"If one advances confidently, (remember tentative lacks power) in the direction of his dreams, and endeavors to live the life he has imagined, he will meet with success unexpected in common hours."**

Clear vision and unshakable faith are critical components of the success formula. Be mindful also that the bridge we must all cross is called "organized action". Keep in mind the words of Aristotle to his students: *"A vivid imagination compels the whole body to obey it."* Therefore, combine "focus" with "action".

Now, envision yourself with plenty of surplus money, month after month. How would you feel about yourself? What could you do for your loved ones that the lack of extra money prevents you from doing right now? Write it on paper! Expect to accomplish what you have written and never lose your focus. What new and exciting experiences could you be engaging in, if money was available for you to choose them? Picture it all happening for you! ***Leave "Survival Street" and start driving on "Prosperity Highway"!***

Maintain the right mental attitude at all times. Always remember that nothing can stop the person with the right mental attitude from achieving his or her goal. Nothing on earth can help the person with the wrong mental attitude to achieve anything worthwhile, let alone financial independence.

Get yourself on a winning team! Don't settle for a seat on the sidelines, watching the game being played, while you're only participating as a critic or a cheerleader. No! Jump off the bench. Get out on the field of action. See what you are really made of. Like the great Gretsky said, **"You miss 100% of the shots you never take!"** As always, the mirror reflects back at the face before it. What is it saying to you?

I choose to see someone who starts their day knowing what is pulling them into action; their clearly defined objectives. I see someone who surrounds themselves with "support wells" to drink from; the right people, CD's, and books. I see someone who is constantly open to the coaching that is available to him or her from those who have accomplished more than they have in business and life. And lastly, I see someone who does not get stuck doing things that he or she likes to do. Instead, I see someone who is doing what those who have succeeded before them have done and are still doing.

## Insight:

**When all is said and done, in life, as well as business, the difference between those who "will have" and those who "will have not", will be clearly traced back to those who "did" and those who "did not"!**

# *Chapter 20 - Success -The Uncommon Understanding*

I have not found in all my years, a single success of magnitude that was devoid of difficulties, risk, disappointments and periods of self-doubt. The road to success is an obstacle course that is laden with emotional ups and downs as one encounters the naysayers, the broken promises, and the quitters; those who professed so much in the beginning and delivered so little in the end. It appears that we achieve our goals in life to the degree that we are able to overcome the negatives. Sophocles said it this way: **"There is no success without hardship." James Allen said, "He who would achieve much, must endure much." To win we must endure the negatives and keep on going.**

You must learn to consider your invested hard work, focused effort, and the emotional pain you experience after disappointments not as negatives to stop you, but rather as necessary deposits or installment payments for eventual success. Why do this? I'll tell you why! Because getting up after being knocked down is the most essential ingredient in the recipe for success.

If one does not quit, every failure is temporary, and every disappointment is a teacher and a builder of resolve. We humans have a remarkable inner ability to achieve what we firmly commit to and believe possible. **<u>A person of inner conviction is a person of massive power.</u>** The fulfillment of a dream comes to the person who mentally and spiritually accepts the dream as a certain eventual reality. As Franklin Roosevelt said, **"The only limit to our realization of tomorrow's dreams will be the doubts we entertain today."** Success is not without struggle and adversity. Success once achieved more than compensates for whatever one endures to get there.

Shakespeare offered us this insight, **"Sweet are the uses of adversity; which like the toad, ugly and venomous, wears yet a precious jewel in his head."**

Now that we understand with each difficulty is a hidden opportunity, what is next? Concentrated effort! We need to gather our scattered forces into one powerful and focused channel. We must focus our efforts on a definite goal. Then, continuously direct your thinking and actions toward the achievement of your goal.

You must rule out all outside influences that do not have a direct bearing on achieving your goal. Therefore, you must guard against associations of thoughts, and with persons, when either is incompatible with your goal. Let no person or no circumstance diminish your resolve to succeed. When you eliminate the distractions and the detractors, you sharpen your focus, and that alone greatly increases your chances for success.

You will need courage when you are discouraged. You must reach deep into your resolve tank and convince yourself that you are more powerful inside than any outside circumstance. **<u>Always be mindful that the most significant battles you will encounter along the road to success will be waged in your mind and with your emotions</u>.** It is here where you will win or lose the battle. Remember also what Emerson wrote, **"Nothing external to you has any power over you."** You simply must not let your mind be subdued or defeated by the obstacles you are sure to encounter. The battleground will always be in your mind. We all win or lose in that arena.

And, finally, you must be realistic with your expectations. There is no sudden leap to success. Our success lies in what we do day after day in an organized and focused way. Little by little is how success is built. If it comes to you it will be the result of small efforts repeated over time toward a firmly desired objective.  Success demands time to evolve.  It comes to those who patiently and bravely endure.  We really do have the power to realize that which we firmly desire and believe possible.  <u>**So, keep on, keepin' on!  Believe in your objective, but most of all believe in yourself!**</u>

## Insight:

Stand firm in you resolve and you'll transform your personal possibility into your reality.  If you can do this, everything you need to become successful is out there waiting to join your efforts.  So, go forth with undaunted enthusiasm and determination knowing that you shall, in the end, be victorious!

## *Chapter 21 - Triumph Over Adversity*

None of us welcome adversity with open arms, yet it is adversity that offers us the chance to endure and learn valuable lessons. These lesson in turn prepare us for eventual success.

Often times the intensity of the struggle to overcome adversity is matched by the bigness of the opportunity on the other side of adversity.

To excel in any endeavor of worth, one has to have a conquering attitude and the ability to control negative impulses— which accompany all struggles and frustrations. With the right mindset and the patience to endure, you can expect to eventually be the winner over adversity.

The conqueror knows that adversity is the single greatest cause of attrition for the masses, those who always seem to fall short of the goal. The winner keeps focused on the possibilities while struggling with adversity; the losers shift their focus to the adversities. And, in so doing, lose their will to endure and press through. When people, events, or circumstance rain on your parade, you need to have an "attitude umbrella" that helps you maintain a sense of purpose and renewed focus on the big picture of what you are trying to achieve. The study of great accomplishments finds the successes were all accompanied by the stories of people who succeeded in spite of severe and often times enduring difficulties.  To become successful, they saw it would be necessary for them to accept that problems arise and then, simply rise above them.  The winners in life have learned to resist the natural urge of frustration when things are not going well.  Know that frustration is a first cousin to anger, and anger is the father of anxiety, who in turn is the brother of frivolous and often counter productive thoughts and actions.  Winners weather the storms of frustration and the dry seasons of labor precisely because they know, in so doing, they will eliminate most of the competition.

Providence itself gets behind the visionary, the person who stays the course when things get difficult.  In this universe of ours **Perseverance and Determination** alone are omnipotent.  Most people who start but never finish the race ignore this one elemental truth.  Circumstances are not always what we might wish for, but there is always a choice in how we react to circumstance.  The winners in life stay the course of what they started and do so with courage, faith, and determination until they become victorious.  I'll close with the words of Harriet Stowe when she said  **"When you find yourself in a tough space and everything seems to be going against you, and it seems as though you can not hang on a minute longer, never give up then, for that is just the place and time that the tide will turn."**

**<u>Insight:</u>**
      **In the final analysis, success will prove to be a matter of hanging on, after others have let go.**

## *Chapter 22 - About Emotions*

Life is a magnificent gift from the creator of all life, an opportunity to join the eternal growth process that this life offers each of us. I can guarantee you that a philosophy that "Life is a struggle, life is hard" will produce exactly that kind of experience of life. Growing, as a person is only a struggle for the person who resists the emotions appropriate to all growth processes. "It's okay to experience negative emotions but it's not okay to be run by them." Each of us experience a life fashioned by our thoughts, emotions, beliefs, and attitudes. Therefore, we generally live the life we are looking for either consciously or unconsciously. The so called 'Good Life" is a life of continuous quest for personal growth….a work in process; a process never finished.

### Let's explain negative emotions

Negative emotions are agitated physical and psychological responses to stimuli that come from our own observations of things we deem unpleasant, not okay, or bad. They result from our own judgments about the things happening in our experience. The vast majority of negative emotions are stimulus/response in nature. That is, they are one's habitual way of thinking and responding to certain events or conditions.

These responses were learned in the past and then stored in the unconscious, waiting to be stimulated by another event or circumstance that resembles the initial episode wherein the emotional response was formulated.

The expression of negative emotions always betrays underlying attitudes. These expressions consist of gestures, body postures, facial expressions, vocal expressions, modulations of voice, etc.

Negative emotions have a vastly different impact on the mind and body organs than do positive emotions like love, joy, happiness, enthusiasm, etc. Negative emotions tear down the body's overall resistance and predispose it to both physical and emotional illness. We learned our negative responses. Therefore, we can learn to replace them with either neutral or positive responses.

Once we understand that we are essentially powerless over others and the way they think and react, we are well on the road to mastery of emotional response. Our negative emotions have their root development in our wanting things to be other than the way they presently are. It's really sort of funny, when you step back and observe yourself reacting negatively to something that "already is" and which nothing can be done to undo. Thus, out of frustration about our powerlessness regarding what "already is", we react!

You can have a life of incredible satisfaction by including your emotions, all your emotions and vulnerability, as an integral part of who you are. Satisfaction in life lives on the other side of where most of us stop. We will do anything to avoid the experience of negative emotions. We've never been taught that it's okay to experience negative emotions and to include them responsibly as an integral part of being alive.

We have learned quite well, however, to be guarded, suppressed, and covert about our true feelings. Society offers us little room to express our true feelings, so most people become "repression machines" and we build up internal pressures that eventually bleed out as disguised half-truths and frustrations.

If you could take a view of your emotions as clever little power brokers, each trying to control your behavior by deceiving you about their power over you, perhaps then you could see yourself taking a stand and confronting them. To confront emotions is not to resist them but rather to experience them and include them as okay.

**If you resist your emotions you are run by them, for that which you resist simply persists.** Your resistance gives inappropriate power to your emotions. In fact, you are unconsciously always engaged with your resisted emotions by making sure you never encounter any aspect of life where you might feel emotions that are not okay for you to feel.

You have, therefore, made a treaty with yourself to do whatever it takes to avoid the experience of negative emotions and now your mind has agreed to shut you off from literally thousands of marvelous opportunities and experiences. Your mind then works to avoid those emotions you've categorized as bad, negative or not okay. Let's consider the following illustration to see how emotions can affect us.

John asked Mary for a date. Mary is very pretty and John is afraid she may not be interested in him (he is fearful of being rejected.) John asks Mary to go out and Mary says, 'No, I'm not interested, thank you."

John now feels the emotion of rejection. He doesn't like the way it feels so he draws some conclusions and makes some judgments about the whole experience. He then stores his conclusions and thoughts deep within his unconscious mind.

Here's what it probably looks like to John:
1. "Pretty girls reject me."
2. "I'll never ask another one out."
3. "I don't deserve a pretty girl."
4. "I must be unlovable."

From these conclusions John now must create a protective mindset that shuts out any experience where he might experience rejection. In other words, John now has an issue with rejection, period!

The issue does not stay focused on pretty girls. John's subconscious understands clearly now that John does not want to be rejected, so it accommodates him by signaling any and all situations where rejection might show up.

Now, just think about how much shutting down must take place if John is to be successful at avoiding rejection. Avoiding rejection now becomes an operating principle, which John is always consciously or unconsciously engaged with.

Now, let's have John use this very same negative emotional experience to empower him to get what he wants.

John asks Mary for a date and Mary says, "No, I'm not interested, thank you." John feels the emotion of rejection and he doesn't like it but he does not conclude the same things about what it means to him. Instead, John asks Betty, another pretty girl, out for a date and continues to ask pretty girls until finally one says, "Yes, John, I'd love to go out with you!"

This is quite a different outcome. John never took the rejection personally. He was not stopped by the rejection but instead; he simply kept asking pretty girls until one said "yes!" John got what he wanted because he included rejection as part of the process of getting a date with a pretty girl. John will never again be afraid to ask a pretty girl for a date. He was actually empowered by including the emotion of rejection as okay.

I will leave you with a powerful contemplation.

**AFFIRMATION**: From this day forward I shall responsibly include the experience of all my emotions and no longer let my mind's desire to avoid them control me or stop me from getting what life has to offer me. Fill out the emotional blocks on the last page of the workbook. Once you identify them, include them!

### What are the most destructive emotions?

- **Doubt**
- **Guilt**
- **Loneliness**
- **Fear**
- **Depression**
- **Shame**
- **Hate**
- **Jealousy**
- **Envy**
- **Resentment**
- **Anger**
- **Self-pity**

### Insight:

**If you can master your emotional responses, you can master this business!**

# *Chapter 23 - The Power Of Personal Integrity*

 If a person of integrity possesses the qualities of goodness, honorableness, morality, righteousness, and virtue, then what would a person who lacks integrity be defined as? Simply, one who lacks these qualities!

Genuine integrity never implies, nor does it accept compromise. Its only judge is the highest standard of truthfulness in all matters. Integrity is not compromised by the guise of situational ethics. No, it stands for what is right, regardless of gain or loss.

It never looks back to think what might have been gained had standards been compromised. Feeling remorse for the person of integrity is saved for the few times he/she might have succumbed to lowering the bar for some personal gain. And, the remorse is deep and heartfelt because a person of integrity is aware that he/she traded a part of their character for a "piece of silver". Their remorse is haunting because their awareness is high, which in turn serves to strengthen one's resolve to never fall again.

Integrity is never boastful because it is aware of its own fragile nature. It strives to become pervasive in the consciousness of people desiring to live a life of honesty and genuine commitment to what is right.

Integrity demands constant vigilance against the many deceptive lures that promise one personal or financial gain through unethical means. Beware that whatever is gained by unethical means is a disguised time bomb of self-imposed destruction, demanding eventual retribution. In retrospect, the undeserved glory or benefit of the gain will pale in comparison to the real price you will repay as the clock moves forward. There is no greater price to pay then to trade, for ill-gotten gain, the essence of your character, your innate potential for goodness, and your serenity of mind and spirit.

The "pillow" is hard for the person who lacks integrity. It is soft and comfortable for the one who possesses it. Sleep is restless for the person who lacks integrity and oh so peaceful for that person who maintains his integrity. Psychological  repression of guilt is ever present in the person who lacks integrity, but not at all present in the person who possesses it. And, if one is no longer bothered by their misdeeds done to others or by dishonesty in their business dealings, then that person is unwittingly paying the biggest price of all-----they must be constantly running from themselves, always watching for new quick fixes and new victims to prey upon. They are living in the quagmire of self-deception and self-imposed ignorance, which always must come face-to-face with those moral laws that demand eventual retribution. There is no escape, only a "stay of execution."

Man is not always immediately punished "for" his misdeeds, but you can count on the fact that he will always be punished "by" his misdeeds. Justice is often a very insidious paymaster. She is not always quick to act, but in some fashion or another, she will always act, but in her own time and way.

A wise person will always place personal integrity at the top of the list of desired virtues for she alone is the custodian of all other virtues.

Personal integrity is your power-base to build all other honorable character traits upon; those traits that build true champions!  Personal integrity will prove to be the best friend you'll ever have as you go through life.  She will always hold your self-esteem at the highest level.   She will allow you to stand tall in adversity, and humble in victory.   Remember this—we grew the character we possess today, one thought, one emotion, and one behavior at a time.   The nature and content of each thought, emotion, and behavior, over time, has fashioned the person we are right now.   To become better, we must think, choose, and behave better.

## Insight:

**Know this!   We can each build a new and better character but only with one correct moral decision at a time. I promise you that you will never regret traveling through life with personal integrity at the helm.**

## *Chapter 24 - Self-Image and Success*

**Probably the biggest trap or pitfall in life is self-doubt or low self-esteem**. It is a psychological pit designed and dug by our own minds. But, we constantly blame its development on others.

Life's most pathetic expression is, "I can't do that!" Defeatism kills your self-image. Even losing after a good fight raises self-esteem. Your self-image sets the boundaries of your accomplishments. Your mental picture of yourself is the real key to understanding your own personality and behavior. All of your actions, feelings, and behaviors, including your abilities, are always consistent with your self-image. You attract conditions in your life that are consistent with your self-image.

Each of us was engineered for happiness and success. Your unconscious mind is absolutely impersonal. It operates as a machine and has no "will" of its own. It works only upon the data which you feed it in the form of ideas, beliefs, opinions, judgments, and interpretations. You developed your own reaction patterns. You learned those patterns, and you can learn new ones. Your present negative beliefs were formed by thoughts plus feelings.

You can think new thoughts and feel new feelings.

Positive thinking does not change the beliefs one has about oneself. Positive thinking works best when it is working with an improving self image.

Your present state of self-esteem is the result of past experiences, which formed thoughts and impressions. The thoughts about the experiences were then interpreted to mean something (which produced feelings), and finally, based upon emotions you felt, you formed your judgments, which you etched in stone to become your self-image.

Quit meditating on your phobias and shortcomings. Learn to be indifferent to your old thinking and reaction patterns. Seek the truth! The truth is, you are far more capable than anything you've accomplished to date indicates.

Esteem means to appreciate the worth of. We stand in awe of the stars, the sea, the sunset, the beauty of a flower and then downgrade the greatest creation, **OURSELVES**.

As you create a better self-image you will discover new abilities, talents, and powers; that will release and utilize what is already lying dormant within you, but yet to be realized, developed, and expressed.

Accept yourself as you are, and start from there. Learn to emotionally tolerate imperfection in yourself. Don't get down on yourself because you're not perfect. You are "Somebody Special", NOW! Accept yourself! Be yourself! Don't turn your back on "you"! It's the only "you" in the game. Live your life with zest, keenness, and a gusto that surmounts obstacles and brushes aside discouragement. Take the lid off and play full out. You'll discover your true self when you do.

**AFFIRMATION: I accept fully the responsibilities for my own thoughts about myself. I accept that I must open myself to new experiences if I am to develop as a person. I forgive everyone (parents, friends, and teachers) who ever told me I couldn't do it.**

**I accept myself as a person of great, untapped potential; forever capable of growing and expanding in service to others and myself. I accept the responsibility to become all that I am capable of becoming. I am committed to being "Awake" and "Alive" from this day forward.**

### Insight:

**"Our deepest fear is not that we are inadequate. Our deepest fear is that we are powerful beyond measure. It is our light, not our darkness that frightens us most. Your playing small does not serve the world." Marianne Williamson**

# *Chapter 25 - Leadership*

As a leader you must be able to motivate people. MOTIVATION consists of essentially 4 phases.

1. You must become skilled at recognizing and bringing to the surface, conversationally, the needs of the individual.
2. You must then learn how to change those needs into "wants" by creating a burning desire for wants.
3. You must provide the individual with the MEANS of satisfying those wants.
4. You must support the person you enrolled with integrity and sincerity and with a style and method that shifts totally the responsibility for achievement to the person who "wants" and away from yourself.

Support is not doing for another, but rather showing another what and how to do for themselves. How one performs is dependent on several interrelated factors. Attitude, skills, knowledge, rewards offered, support given, and the environment in which one lives and works are the principle factors which influence performance. As a leader you must always consider and evaluate the impact of these factors on the individual.

## To be an effective leader:

1. You must be totally committed to your company and your product.
2. You must accurately define your goals. Your people must define and believe they can attain their own goals.
3. You must provide a practical and definite Plan of Action that has exacting functions to be performed daily, weekly, and monthly.
4. You must monitor your progress and meet regularly with your people to discuss options, make necessary adjustments and modifications and to praise and motivate them for what they've done to date.
5. You must be willing to do, on a consistent basis, more than anyone else in your organization.
6. You must love your people, even if you don't like the things they are doing or failing to do!

Be sure to utilize the Leadership Training in Section 6.

## Insight:

**Your leadership development will prove to be the foundation of your success and satisfaction in your business. Make it a learning priority!**

# *Chapter 26 - Preparation Pays*

Let me illustrate the value of proper preparation. John and Bill are both starting their sales careers as new representatives on the same date. Both have been advised to study their presentation materials for a minimum of 12 hours before rushing out to talk to prospects. Both have made a prospect list of 100 potential customers from the same basic groupings of acquaintances. Both appear equal in all aspects except one. John studied and mastered his presentation and Bill decided to "wing it". Let's see the outcome. Statistics indicate that a well planned, informative, and sales directed presentation will out-perform the "wing it" approach at a 4 to 1 presentation to close ratio. This simply means that the prepared representative will close 4 times the rate of the representative that is" winging it, if they are doing the same amount of presentations. This equals 4 times the income. The difference is preparation.

**PREPARATION before performance is the key!**

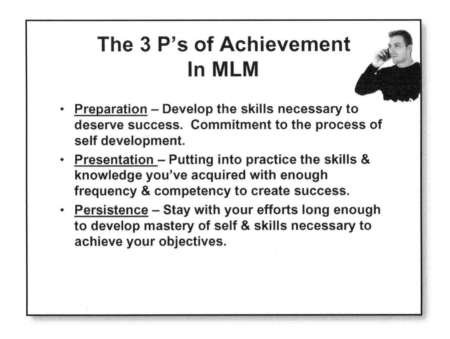

**Insight:**

If you are not committed to preparation you are committed to failure!!!

# *Chapter 27 - About Time*

**Where does your time go?**
**ACTIVITY (Averages)**
**Sleeping- 8 hours**
**Personal Hygiene – 1 hour**
**Eating – 3 hours**
**Going to and from work – 2 hours**
**Working – 8 hours**
**TOTAL - 22 hours**

This leaves two hours per day for five days or 10 hours, Monday through Friday, to do all the other things that you need or want to do. Theoretically, then, you have about 20 hours on weekends to do other fun or creative things that energize you and make life enjoyable.

So managing your time is managing your life.

### 10 Steps to Time Management
1. Analyze how you use your time now,
2. Decide what the best use of your time is.
3. Organize your time.
4. Control time wasters.
5. Use time savers.
6. Establish priorities.
7. Don't major in minor things.
8. Learn the value of saying "no".
9. Learn to make decisions.
10. DO IT NOW

## Recommendations

- The best way to overcome time-wasting habits is to acquire the habit of SCHEDULING.
- Block out PLANNING TIME.
- Make a HABIT of doing A and B above. To replace old habits with new ones requires an understanding of the dynamics of habit. Failure habits are easier to acquire than they are to break, so you will need a lot of resolve and commitment.
- Identify your self-defeating habits. Make a list.
- Replace each with contrasting habits.
- Practice the new habits daily for 30 consecutive days until they are firmly rooted.
- Be fully aware that a tendency to act — to use our new behavior becomes effectively ingrained as new habit only in proportion to the frequency with which the action actually occurs.
- Newton's Law of Inertia says, "A body at rest tends to remain at rest and a body in motion tends to remain in motion." Pick one!
- Always give yourself exacting deadlines.
- Remember, as Ralph Waldo Emerson wrote, **"Success depends on a plus condition of mind and body, on power of work, and on courage."**
- No rule for success will work if you won't.

## Managing Time Means...

- The ability to identify important issues and focus on those issues to their conclusion.
- Making tough priority decisions and acting upon them.
- Spending enough time on all the activities necessary to

accomplish your objectives.
- Realizing that you cannot hope to control everything, but that you can certainly control some things.
- Improving those things you can and learning to live with those you cannot.
- Accepting responsibility for your own action and lack of action.
- Living your life on purpose.
- Managing yourself.

## **Procrastination**

Putting off a task is a major barrier to effective time use.

Do you:

- Put things off until the last minute?
- Live by the "better late than never" motto?
- Say you work better under pressure?
- Avoid doing new tasks?
- Hate to start a big job?
- Postpone necessary but unpleasant tasks?
- Avoid jobs where you risk failure?
- Involve yourself in avoidance activities, i.e., excessive sleeping, eating, television watching, daydreaming?

## What holds procrastination together?

## Fear- Anger - Worry -Guilt -Insecurity –Past Failures

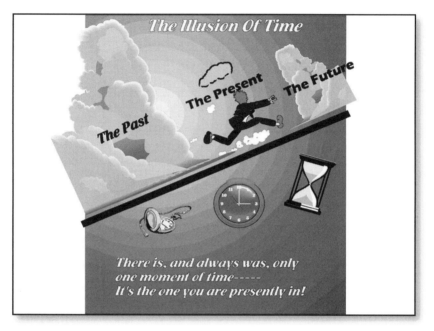

## Insight:

The only moment you have to do any task is really in the moment of NOW. Your life is a moment by moment experience in the NOW. Yesterday is gone, tomorrow is in the future. What you do in the present determines your future. Respect your time as a limited but invaluable resource. If you expect a better tomorrow, you must create it in the continuous moment of NOW!

# *Chapter 28 -About Money*

**People who work for money seldom have much.
People who work for results can create lots of it.**

## Some principles:
- Pay yourself first — Save 10% right off the top.
- Audit your lifestyle, live within your means.
- Don't buy on time. Paying high interest rates is one of the surest ways to never have any money!
- Establish an Emergency Fund of 3 months income.
- You can become financially independent if you start now.
- Contribute to charitable causes – What you give comes back to you.
- Make money your friend.
- Invest in self-improvement on a regular basis.
- Reward yourself for things accomplished.
- If you continue to do what you do now for money, you will get more of what you have now. Do you see a need for a change?

Money is not evil in and of itself, as some have been taught. Money will expand who you already are. It will make a good man better and a bad man worse.

If you have a moral issue with money, then I suggest you make a lot of it and give it to worthy causes!

Most people don't plan to fail; they fail to plan!

Insight:

Most people are heavily in debt because their desire to have things greatly exceeds their desire to do things! For your finances to improve, you must improve!

All financially successful people see the correlation between having money and the work required to justify having the money!

# *Chapter 29 - Goals*

The first step to goal setting is a process of taking truthful stock of you. Just what are your personal and business goals? Fill out the worksheet on goals in the back of this book. Are you really satisfied with where you are and what you've accomplished to date? Tell the truth. The truth avoided is still the truth. It's a passive decision to do nothing about your situation.

If life is to have meaning it must have a purpose. And to fulfill a purpose you need goals and an activity plan to follow. Setting goals is serious business and should be taken seriously. Psychologists tell us that the vast majority of people never take the time to sit down and figure out who they are and what they want out of life. Most people reach mid-life before they admit they haven't done much goal setting at all.

A major university studied alumni 20 years after graduation. Only 3% of them had established clear lifetime goals, monitored their activities to support their intentions, and stayed true to their commitments. This 3% had accomplished more than all the other 97% combined. We need to convince ourselves that there is time to reverse the tide and then modify our expectations upward.

We can shift to higher levels of achievement by setting and committing to specific activity goals. That's the key! The destination of any journey is reached by accomplishing one step (activity) at a time. The result (goal) is already guaranteed to us if we engage in the supporting activities that get us there. The secret is no secret at all — simply take a stand with your spoken intentions (written goals), and commit yourself to accomplishing what you set out to do.

Let nothing stop you. Don't let unpleasant feelings stop you, i.e., frustration, fatigue, anxiety, rejection, inadequacy, helplessness, loneliness. Negative emotions are self-imposed feelings we engage with, in order to justify breaking our commitments. All winners have learned to include the experience of negative emotions, but not in a disempowering way. They integrate them as part of the success experience.

You were designed by nature as an achievement machine. One, however, that is free to choose to achieve or not to achieve. The wise person understands this. Set specific goals! They are absolutely essential!!

Engage with specific supporting activities! Don't ever quit! **Quitting is the ultimate defeat of the human personality.** It becomes a habitual way of responding to life's challenging situations. You have the inherent capabilities to be successful. Yes, they must be nurtured and developed through application and practice, but the point is: you have them. Nobody ever became a winner by trying something half-heartedly.

The winners in any walk of life took a stand for what they wanted to accomplish and went to bat often enough to be able to hit the ball. The best of them, at their peak of performance, succeed only about one third of the time, and they are champions. All winners clearly learn how to include failure as part of being successful. You can too, if you don't allow the experience of uncomfortable emotions to steal your dreams.

Set up your target, organize your plan of attack, get determined, and get into action. Success always responds to that kind of commitment.

In connection with goal setting most of us are prone to underestimate ourselves and our abilities, and overestimate the difficulties facing us.

**Decide what you want — NOT what you DON'T want!**

Concentrate your thinking on what you want and pay strict attention to the task at hand, and trust the desired result will eventually show up. Results take care of themselves!

Dr. William James, Dean of American psychologists, gave us a deep insight when he said, **"When once a decision is reached [the goal is set] and execution [activity plan] is the order of the day, dismiss absolutely all responsibility and care about the outcome. Unclamp, in a word, your intellectual and practical machinery, and let it run free; and the service it will do you will be twice as good."**

Success comes as a result of personal surrender to your purpose (goal). In other words, give your resistant "struggle and effort" self a rest, and let the greater self take over. You can abandon stressful effort and accomplish with ease that which has eluded you thus far if you can grasp and put to use this insight. Nothing can resist a clearly defined intention of a human being who has surrendered to that intention or goal.

**The key again is surrender to purpose. Negative emotions which cause most people to quit are simply not engaged with in the same crippling way by the person who is surrendered to purpose. They do not stop these people, but actually empower them to go on. The negative emotions are**

not resisted but included. It's okay to feel them, but it's not okay to let them stop you. Reread this section until you feel the shift of insight that says, "I own it now! I've found the key!"

## THE POWER OF MENTAL FOCUSING:

When you want a thing in your life, picture it as already present in every detail. Hold that image resolutely in your mind. Now include absolute faith that you will possess it and you can fully expect the necessary energy, action, and steadfast courage to bring into your reality the very thing that you want.

The true and intense desires of your mind and heart become magnetized to the conditions and ingredients needed to create what it is you have commanded to be yours.

What you genuinely ask for must come to pass if you picture it long enough, clearly enough, and confidently enough.

You have the power to literally materialize your thoughts!

### Insight:
You can't hit a target if you don't have a target you declared and intend to hit. Decide what you want and then do what's required of you to get it.

# *Chapter 30 - Performance Schedule*

Here's a Performance Schedule to get you where you want to go. Simply make an initial commitment for 30 days to achieve 10 performance points each day. If you break your commitment on the 15th day, you must start all over again until you have 30 consecutive working days in an unbroken link of achieving a minimum of 10 performance points. The results you will produce by using this method will prove one of two very interesting things:

1. You will discover the key to achievement is setting goals, performing supporting activities, and consistency. You will also discover the awesome power of keeping your word.

OR

2. You will discover you don't have the business you'd like to have, which will be nothing more than discovering you have not kept your commitment for 30 days. After you have kept your performance commitment for 30 consecutive days see if you want to continue or not. You will discover you want to continue.

## Daily 10 Point Must System-Activity points

**Sell a product- 3 pts**
**Sponsor a new business builder- 5pts**
**Make new recruiting appointment- 4pts.**
**Present business opportunity - 3 pts**
**Conduct a meeting in your home- 7 pts**
**Attend a meeting- 3pts**
**Bring a guest to a business meeting (each guest-) 3pts**
**Conduct a meeting in someone else's home- 4pts**
**Attend a national conference- 10pts**

**Every day 10 Performance Points for 30 consecutive days will create momentum in your business!**

**<u>Insight</u>:**

To avoid these required activities is to invite failure. It is not good enough that we do what we feel good doing or like to do.  In our business, we have to do what is required.

# Section 3 –
# Critical Insights
# for Success

# *Chapter 31 - The 10 Commandments of Becoming Successful in Network Marketing*

1. Thou shalt not expect others to do what you are no longer doing to expand your business.
2. Thou shalt not buy into or linger with other people's negative comments or attitudes.
3. Thou shalt not dwell on the past nor continue to linger with thoughts of what should have happened, but did not happen.
4. Thou shalt not get frustrated or angry when people do not do what they say they are going to do. Many don't.
5. Thou shalt not expect the company to never make mistakes because occasionally it will.
6. Thou shalt face each problem you or your distributors encounter as a leader and demonstrate a calming influence to your group and not spearhead hostile and accusatory complaining.
7. Thou shalt continue to sponsor new first level representatives as an example for your organization to follow.
8. Thou shalt continue to concentrate on those distributors in your group who are working hard and possess the correct attitudes for success.
9. Thou shalt set specific personal performance and income goals and then reach them.
10. Thou shalt reach the next pin level of your company's compensation plan by_____(Date).

**Insight:**
   **You can expect to become successful if you keep these Commandments.**

# *Chapter 32 - Profile of a winner in MLM*

Does the person have the ability to influence people?

Is he or she hungry to grow as a leader?

Are they coachable?

Do they have character?

Are they willing to pay the price for success in order to enjoy the benefits of success?

Do they have a willingness to serve others and support the dreams of others?

Do they have the ability to convince others to attend company sponsored training events?

Here is a graphic of what it takes to build residual income from Network Marketing. Picture the ball at the bottom of the mountain as a huge snowball and you have to get it to the top of the mountain. You will need many helpers along the way to the top. But, once you reach the top of the mountain, the momentum will begin. Your business will grow just like a snowball with the downward momentum of the mountain, increasing your residual income with little or no help from you. You must remember however, that you will certainly lose some of your snowball lifting distributors, as you climb the mountain. So, you must be prepared to continuously add

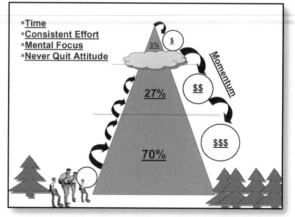

new mountain climbers to increase momentum and lift the snowball to the top. Momentum is created through the efforts and results produced in various lines of sponsorship throughout your organization. **These are the business builders in your organization who are working for their own reasons and income goals.**

You will also notice the numbers on this graphic. They correspond to the statistical averages of most organizations. Three percent of people are true self starters. They are self directed, self responsible and goal oriented. The next group of 27% are hard workers; most have jobs or own their own small business. They have a sincere desire to better their lives. These 2 groups are where your best recruiting results will come from, and mostly from the 27% group. The top 3% usually have their system of producing wealth and only listen to other 3%ers. Occasionally you will find a 3%er in transition and sponsor them. The bottom 70% are mostly skeptical or negative thinkers, almost always work for others, have a survival mentality, and are not committed to personal development. This group will occasionally produce a good representative. Just be quick to decide who deserves your attention and who is not a serious prospect.

**Insight**:

    **In growing your business you will need 4 components.**
1. **Time**
2. **Consistent effort**
3. **Mental focus**
4. **A Never quit attitude**

## *Chapter 33 - Did You Put The Key In The Door?*

This is a very important concept. People are always awakened when I explain this contrast to them. The contrast is the difference between owning a small business in a single location to owning your Network Marketing business with virtually unlimited locations. And, further, you can operate your MLM business from the comfort of your home as opposed to needing a separate piece of real estate confined to a single location. I often use a pizzeria as an example.

First, I go through a long list of business investments you would make to open such a business. You would spend a good deal of time picking out a good location for the shop. If you got a good location, you would have spent quite a bit of money for it. Then you would purchase ovens, refrigerators, kitchen equipment, tables, chairs, plates, glasses, utensils, and napkins. Then, you would need to decorate the dining area and put up a sign advertising your pizzeria. And, of course, purchase the ingredients for your pizzas and accompanying foods. You would need an accountant, liability and property insurance and most likely a lawyer. All of these things would cost money. You are now open for business. Your hours of operation are 12 noon -12 midnight. Can you imagine not coming to work to open your shop until 1pm? What would happen to your reputation if customers came and the Pizzeria was not open? You would not think of doing such a thing because you have such a large investment in your business!! Failure could be financially devastating.

But, in Network Marketing we have a huge upside potential with very small money investments or risk, so we don't take our business as seriously as we should. I maintain if we had to invest the same money a traditional business requires to open, we would be sure to do the actions required to be successful! So, I encourage you all to ask yourself everyday, "Did I put the key in the door today?" In business you must!! Now go back and review your commitment to the daily 10 point must system under the article Performance Schedule. This is how you put the key in the door of a Network Marketing business!

**Insight:**
**Everyday you have countless occasions to offer your opportunity to others. So be ready and alert and seize those opportunities. Those who show, grow!**

## *Chapter 34 - The Champions Success Formula*

This condenses the formula for success. **First, you must clearly define you reason for doing the business.** Define it in detail. Use the back of this book to write your goals down. Make a declaration to yourself and significant others what your intention is, along with a time line for achieving it. You must keep yourself focused on your declared intention or goal. As you work toward the goal, you will develop your skills; presentation skills, inviting people to your meetings, selling your product, coaching skills, sponsoring, and public speaking. During this time, it is imperative that you keep a good attitude and continue with the actions of selling your product and sponsoring new people. If you persist in doing these actions and behaviors you

**The Champion's Success Formula**

- <u>Intention</u>-What am I after?

- <u>Declaration</u> - I fully intend to get there!

- <u>Focus</u> - Mind Alignment

- <u>Skill Development</u> - Identify weaknesses

- <u>Action</u> - Employing the necessary attitudes and behaviors to win

- <u>Persistence</u> - The driving force behind success

will be successful! An important section on your motivators and de-motivators is in the back of this book on three pages.

You must identify which are your personal motivators and de-motivators and stay consciously aware of them. Add power to your key motivators and conquer your de-motivators!

# *Chapter 35 - Understanding Persistence*

The best way for me to teach persistence is with the following picture. You see the last 10% of your time and effort will produce 90% of your results. People simply quit too soon. Let me illustrate this for you by using an American basketball player, Michael Jordan, as an example. When Michael was in High School, he did not, at first attempt, get chosen as a team member. He was told if he practiced and got better he might get to play the next year. As Michael progressed in his sport, he got to play on his High School team. Then, he played for his College team. All this time that Michael was practicing in High School and College, he did not earn any money. After college, he went on to play as a professional. Now Michael started to make a fortune playing his sport. Then, more big money came from his endorsements of basketball shoes, T-shirts and everything else he promotes. This came after many years of playing as a professional and showing his value. But, what if he had quit when he was in High School being told he wasn't good enough? In any endeavor, what creates success is learning, applying, improving, skill sharpening, and more learning.

Many of the greatest achievers of all time were told they were not good enough at some point. But, they persisted until they reached their objective. **However, they all possess these 4 traits:**

- **Intense desire to succeed!**
- **Refusing to let failure stop them!**
- **Enduring great ridicule and rejection!**
- **Persisting until they reached their objective!**

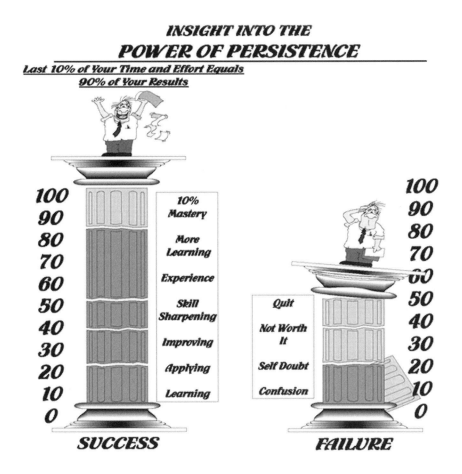

**Insight:**

**Persistence is what transforms a person of ordinary ability into a person of extra-ordinary achievement.**

# Section 4
# Articles To Encourage You

## *Chapter 36 - From Faith To Power!*

You!  Yes, I mean **you** are as powerful as **you** believe and allow yourself to be!  The key word here is "believe."

Most people never break the chains of self-limiting thoughts because they have chosen to identify themselves as a person who is not at all consistent with their true potential.  Most people have internalized the opinions of others as being an accurate identity of themselves.

We humans have great difficulty accepting the fact that the world without is a replica of the world within.  And, the world within creates through our thoughts, emotions, and attitudes, the world we experience without.  It follows therefore, that one's emotions and attitudes manifest in the choices of behaviors that follow the dictates of one's thoughts.  Thought dictates, and emotion, attitude and behavior blindly obey.  Therefore, the only way to create a different opinion or outcome is to change the nature and content of your thoughts.  For example, the thought "I could never be a great salesperson, teacher, or public speaker" produces the feelings and emotions of "incapable, not good enough, incompetent, stupid, unworthy, inadequate, etc., etc." This, in turn, creates an attitude of "I'm inferior to the task" which is followed by the behavior of "rejecting involvement" or even trying.  Unless this thought pattern changes there is zero chance of that person ever becoming a good salesperson, teacher, or public speaker.

As children, we fell down very often before we began to walk upright. But, we kept on getting up and trying. And, what was the end result? We eventually walked and did so very efficiently. Why? It was because we had no history of past failures or opinions of others that could influence our opinions of our own capabilities. In  fact, we had parents, grandparents, and others, encouraging and applauding our efforts to keep going until we were successful. You see, the truth was all along that you were designed by nature to be capable of walking. That capability (potentiality) was with you at birth, but you did not notice that nature demanded that you develop that skill by trial and error. She was teaching you right from the beginning of your life "to get to success you must go through failure!" The "truth" of your ability to walk however, was only unquestionably manifest to you by your personal direct experience of actually walking.

Most of us would still be crawling on all fours had nature set it up that we had to learn how to walk when we were thirty or forty years old. Why? Because by that age, we would have experienced many failures in life, and had many super-imposed limiting opinions of others that we had internalized. In addition, we would have seen others trying to walk, and having observed them falling, and sometimes even getting bruised or gashed, and it would have made us fearful to try. You see, fear of failure would create reluctance to try. **And, reluctance to trying is the great thief of personal achievement and happiness.**

Have you noticed that everything in nature is demonstrating

its potentiality to become something other than how it started? Nature demands growth from all her subjects. When there is no more growth, there is a diminishing of life. What follows over time is eventual death. Or, upon a closer look, a transformation into building blocks for something else, still expressing its desire for life and growth. Nature speaks to humans in a harsh, but caring voice-----**"Don't you dare rust out; keep on working, playing, enjoying, and growing until you wear out!**

To be fully complete in life, we need to be fully involved. And, to be fully involved we need to know our true nature. Only then can we know our true capabilities as humans. What we need is a "Direct Experience" of our true nature which is god-like and therefore, inherently very capable of creating, expressing, and growing as we choose. Each of us shares in the omnipresent, all powerful, loving energy of the Creator of our Universe. There is no object or place that could exist without this participation. With humans, however, it is all a matter of degrees. All other things or creatures on the planet participate by design or inherent program; but we humans participate by choice. We each determine our own level of belief and participation. We participate initially by the courage of faith, and only later through direct experience.

We live very comfortably by faith each and every day, but we hardly notice. We have faith that a green traffic light for us is a red light for another. We drive on. We have faith that the foods we eat every day are devoid of poison. We eat confidently every day. We have faith that when the dial on the stove says off, that it is off. We leave our homes confident that there will be no fire. Yet, we lack faith in the fact that we are god-like in nature.

You see a faith devoid of doubt lives beyond logic or intellectual gymnastics. Your mind may never provide you enough evidence to take the initial leap of faith. That is why it is called faith. The knowing comes, not from the mind, but from the source of the mind, the spirit, which is directly connected to the "Source"; of which most of us call God or Supreme Being.

When belief and faith pervades your consciousness, what follows is increased confidence and decisiveness of action. This is where one acts as though it is impossible to fail. Your thoughts and attitudes transcend limitations. Your focus sharpens, and your energy seems boundless. You are connected! You become a magnetic force attracting the knowledge, people and inspiration to assist you on your journey toward the accomplishment of your purpose or goal.

Your dreams are no longer dreams of hope or longing. They instead become blueprints for the action, attitudes, and circumstances you will need to create to accomplish your desired end.

In order for all this to become "true" for us, we will need to get our heads out of the way! We need to put our hearts and spirits at the controls because they are the real connections to your true God-like nature.

And, remember this! We all start this journey in FAITH, but as the journey progresses you will witness enough solid evidence to convince also your mind that this is who you were all along. So, get to know who you really are and live the rest of your life demonstrating it!

## Insight:

"True faith is not a blind leap in the dark, but rather a true search for light that illuminates the path you need to take to materialize that which you believe in without needing proof in the present." *George Zalucki*

# *Chapter 37 - Am I Climbing up Or Am I Falling Down?*

If you want to reach the top of the Network Marketing Mountain, than you'd better learn to climb. The best way to learn how to be a Network Marketing Mountain Climber is to watch, listen, learn, and model the actions of those who have already reached the top. Logical enough, isn't it? Yet, so few actually model those at the top. Most Reps or Distributors do what they feel is enough or what makes them feel comfortable and not what the job demands.

When I observe failure or stagnation in an individual's Network Marketing business, I see the following:

1. Poor preparation and no definite activity plan to follow.
2. Lack of practice and steady improvement of their inviting skills and their one-on-one opportunity presentation skills.
3. A small or nonexistent prospect list.
4. Irregular or no involvement at all in the weekly business opportunity meetings.
5. Seldom, or never, putting prospects on 3-way calls with their upline expert.
6. Inconsistent work ethic toward the opportunity.

7.  Not attending a company sponsored National or International Training Event.
8.  Offering ineffective and poor examples for their group members to follow.
9.  Having a strong tendency to look for the negatives so as to take the focus away from their lack of performance.
10. Lacking the necessary passion and commitment required to reach the top.

**Here are two test questions that will reveal an objective and truthful answer to where each of us stands with regard to our personal passion and commitment to reaching the top of the MLM Mountain.**

- **Q1. If the owners of my MLM company worked like I've been working since I've become involved, would the opportunity still be alive today?**

- **Q2. If everyone in my personal group, and including my upline leader, duplicated exactly my work ethic and level of business building activity, would they be proud to follow my example and call me a good sponsor or leader, or would they consider me a business building farce?**

Conclusion! Network Marketing is a simple business. We only do two things that we need to get good at, and do both with a plan and a fair level of frequency.

1. We offer services and or products to people we know. Often, they are products and services these people are already accustomed to paying for each and every month; and you offer these at affordable prices.

2. We present an income opportunity that offers financial improvement, including true potential for financial independence to the thousands of people out there who need what Network Marketing offers, but are not yet aware of your company.

Simply put, if you are doing enough of one and two above, the rest of what you need to plug into will create a natural vacuum and pull you in. If you truly want to reach the top of the Network Marketing Mountain, just contrast your personal approach, attitudes, and actions against the failing nine items listed on page 22(Traits of a Good Sponsor)and put in the corrections.

## Insight:
**Remember, that nothing is easy for the unmotivated, except failure.**

## *Chapter 38 - Reaching Dream Island*

I am reminded of the words of Goethe- ----**"Until a person is committed, there will be hesitancy, the chance to draw back; the result will always be ineffectiveness."** People of accomplishment know from experience, that the moment one is firmly committed to something, at that very same moment, the Universe moves to assist them.

We must set our dreams in staunch faith, and once set, let our faith destroy the shadows of doubt that will certainly be encountered as we move toward our dreams. Sometimes, your thoughts and emotions may fail you. But, a sustained faith never! If we can start, then we can finish because we can learn what needs to be done as long as we stay true to our initial commitment. Gather mentors to your side by showing your firm and sincere intention to listen, learn, and grow from their instructions and guidance. **Don't lean----Learn, and then, do!** You will soon notice that each positive action you make to support your dreams will greatly overshadow the negatives you are certain to encounter along the way.

The good life, the enlightened life, is one where problems and obstacles are viewed as necessary teachers that expand our knowledge and resolve to win. Be mindful as you journey to success, that there will be temptation to skepticism and despair. But, be mindful also that these two "killers of dreams" have sent millions back to a life of mediocrity and chronic apathy. As you pass through the days and months ahead, you will come to a place in your mind and spirit where you will recognize that the real journey you've undertaken was clearly a pilgrimage of self-discovery. Allow your work ethic to sustain you in spite of your bouts with discouragement and periods of self-doubt.

**Don't wait for the "right" mood.  Moods change, and therefore cannot be trusted to sustain the necessary effort to build momentum.  If you rely on your moods to energize your efforts, you will accomplish very little.  <u>Your work will bring you inspiration!</u> So, rely on disciplined, directed activity and you will eventually succeed.**

Know this clearly! You can create the future of your choice! As humans, our creative power is "thought." It is your method of thinking that has created the life you now live. Therefore, it will be "new thinking" that will bring into existence the new life you desire. In having new and exciting dreams for your life, you will find yourself, and also lose yourself, as you journey toward those dreams. As you persevere, you will increase your knowledge and skills that will lead you to victory. Perseverance will eventually, but certainly, attract the teachers, events, as well as the physical and spiritual energies required to materialize your dreams.

Become absorbed in your dreams. Dreams are reality, first in spirit, and eventual reality in material form.  While in spirit, ("thought form"), they are constantly nurtured by faith.

I'll close with the words of Helen Keller.  **"We can do anything we want to, if we stick to it long enough."**  And to this I add---- **"Nothing worthwhile is a cakewalk."**  That being said, I encourage you to become "abnormal" in your dreams and actions. Make the decision to leave mediocrity once and for all and set your sails for "Dream Island". And, of course, you must be certain to put enough sustained wind in your sails to reach Dream Island!

**<u>Insight:</u>**
    **"If we want to change our tomorrows, we must change our today or the rest of our lives will be like our yesterdays!"**
*George Zalucki*

# *Chapter 39 - People Grow Who Show!*

It is interesting to observe the growth differences that exist among Network Marketing Representatives. We all start hearing the very same story; the Company, the Products/Services, and the Compensation Plan. This opportunity "Threesome" is exactly the same for every Representative that signs on to build a business.

One can only conclude from this universal constant which exists for all Reps, that the only variable in the game is the individual representative who signs the application. What is the difference between the person who starts by hearing the story and goes on to become a business and income success, and the person who hears that exact same story but does little with the opportunity? In order to come up with an explanation we must do a proper analysis of the difference that exists in the **Attitudes, Level of Commitment, Coachability, and Work Ethics** of those who become a success or failure. Let's face it, there is really nothing else to analyze beyond these four. They are the fundamental underpinnings of success.

Let me start by listing for you the researched reasons why people stay average or fail in business or life in general, not just Network Marketing . The "Dirty Dozen," which are listed below, will provide clarity on where each of us stands as it relates to building a successful business.

## The Twelve Reasons For Failure
1. Lack of understanding of what success demands.
2. Lack of motivation to learn what is required. (Not setting big enough goals to draw you into sustained action limits your desire and will to persevere.)
3. Little self-discipline - A poor personal work ethic is

the primary cause of money deficiency and business failures.

4. Believing in short cuts. - Doing it your way instead of the proven way and expecting your group to do what you are not doing yourself

5. Lack of Integrity with self and others. - Uses deceptive business practices.

6. Poor Self Image - Get over it! You need to engage in new behaviors that challenge you so that you can believe new positive things about yourself. This is the only way to improve your self-image.

7. Negative Personality. - This is the greatest self-con on the market. Negative people set themselves up as "critics", but seldom do you find them in the trenches, except when you look at their bank balance.

8. Lack of Self-Responsibility. - There is very little hope for the person who does not grow to a vivid awareness that he or she is totally responsible for their successes and failures.

9. Lack of Sustained Effort. - You can never build momentum by letting go of the pump's handle. If you lose its "prime", you will have to start over again.

10. Projects Failures and Shortcomings on Others. - A guaranteed prescription for failure and a life of economic and personal misery.

11. Low Tolerance for discomfort—Emotionally, Financially, and Physically. I have taught you that this is a 100% emotional business. Discomfort is the constant companion of every person striving for a big financial goal. That is the primary reason why there are so few financially free people. Those who make it know that financial rewards follow an extended period of sustained physical and emotional output. Either

one surrenders to these truths, incorporates them into their daily activities, or he is destined to live a life of unfilled dreams and financial survival at best.

12. <u>Resistance to Personal Development and Coaching</u>. This is another self-con game. As long as one resists the notion that "if I expect my life to change then I must change", it will be all but impossible for that person to become successful. Individuals resist this idea because at some psychological level they know that their excuses for not doing well would no longer be valid. They want to avoid a situation where they will be judged by only the results they produce. Their resistance to falling in line with the actions and attitudes of the winners keeps them hidden and not vulnerable to performance analysis. They know if they fully participate they have a chance of winning but they also have a chance of having their weaknesses exposed. And this risk prevents them from going all out.

Well, there you have it – the analysis of why people fail or stay average; the Dirty Dozen of Failure.

It is absolutely amazing to see the simplicity of what actually needs to be done to reach a fantastic level of financial success in MLM, and yet to observe the behaviors, attitudes and work ethics of those who are "groaning but not growing".

## **Here is our business in a nutshell.**
<u>What we do, or do not do, determines the outcome!</u>
- We retail products and/or services.
- We expose the business opportunity to others in order to build a residual income.

- We plug our team reps, and ourselves, into all the support systems available from our company.
- It is clearly obvious that you can't "grow" your business if you don't "show" your business.

## **Therefore, you will not succeed if you are:**

- No longer putting out opportunity CDs or DVDs on a regular basis. (At least 3-5 per week)
- Not inviting people to get on your weekly conference calls and to train your team to conduct in home presentations during the weekdays.
- No longer involving your upline in 3 way recruiting calls.
- No longer attending local, regional, or national meetings. (Corporate National conferences build belief, and commitment to a level unmatched by any other business building activity.)
- Not teaching your personally sponsored representatives the realities.
- Not selling products.

As I said when I started, "The variable is you, it's me!" What needs doing, anyone who wants to, can do! That can't be said about most other traditional business opportunities. They require a no nonsense approach, high skill, educational requirements, combined with sustained effort, defined focus, long hours, and great financial risk.

I am absolutely convinced that if one really understands just how big an MLM opportunity is, and also realizes that the average person can gain enormous financial rewards, there would be a huge shift and improvement in their level of commitment, attitude, coachablilty and personal work ethic. Trust me, not only will that shift in your personal approach to the business prove to be the basis and ultimate cause of your success, but it will also prove to you that there was no other way.

As always, the advice is offered but the consequences of neglecting it carry a huge price and it is called failure. Success is not nearly as hard as most people believe it to be. Simply follow the proven path of those who have made it before you and one day you shall be numbered among them. The fact is, MLM has offered all of us that have signed on a real and proven opportunity to dramatically improve our financial fortunes, up to and including total financial freedom. So why not get it right, do it right, and succeed!

**<u>Insight</u>:**
**"Success" is the "great eraser" of all the pain associated with the challenges we must all face and conquer before prosperity is ours to enjoy. Once there, we will laugh at the past challenges and delight in the fruits of our success. So, if you want to fly to high places, you'd better get out of your comfort cocoon.** *George Zalucki*

# *Chapter 40 - The Top Of The Compensation Plan or Bust*
### *The Required Attitudes and Character Traits*

The top of your compensation plan is a very powerful and financially rewarding position. It is one that will test your mind, body, and spirit before it is yours to own. To reach that position, you will need courage and lots of unwavering determination along the way.

You will need to maintain a positive state of mind, a can do attitude, a capacity to focus on your vision of success, and an unwavering faith in your ability to get there. You will need to be different than most other people in the content and the quality of your character and the intensity of your efforts to achieve.

You will need the capacity to tolerate gracefully, and without lingering, emotional upsets and disappointments with people, and circumstances, those that will discourage the weak and force them out of your business.

You will need to often remind yourself that you are different; you really are tougher than most, and that single quality is your edge. Look at the top representatives that already exist and what you see are common men and women who were willing to be dressed in working clothes for 2-3 years in order to wear tailor made clothes for the rest of their lives. These people all faced many obstacles along their journey to the top. But, unlike the person who falls along the way, these reps's used the obstacles they encountered as stepping stones bringing them closer to their dreams. Albert Einstein said, **"In the middle of difficulty lies opportunity."** And, Winston Churchill said, **"Success is going**

**from failure to failure without loss of enthusiasm."** Ours is a business where ordinary people with ordinary talent can reach the top with extraordinary perseverance.

After 33 years in this Industry, I have made an observation about those people who reach the top, and it is this: "Success is due less to the individuals' abilities but far more to do with their "will to win" and their "attitudes of mind." **"The winners never quit and the quitters never win."**

The winner is Dependable! He/She is conscientious and zealous and can always be counted on to help.

The winner is Honest! Honesty is an attitude of mind and spirit shown by your words and actions as you build your business.

The winner possesses a high level of Integrity! Webster defines integrity as "an uncompromising adherence to a code of moral, artistic, or other values." Another understanding would be as follows: "Integrity indicates a sense of values that gives priority to truth, commitment, reliability, and personal initiative." It is a readiness to scrupulously fulfill obligations, promises, and agreements.

If you possess integrity you can be depended upon to carry out your duties and commitments punctually, even when unwatched and unrewarded. Conversely, the lack of personal integrity is the single most contributing cause of the personal failures in all aspects of one's life.

All too may people fail to realize that failing to do what is required of you when you have the ability to do so, is one of

the biggest breaches of your personal integrity. Making excuses for your lack of business growth, which are untrue, but are instead a cover-up for your lack of real effort is another breach of your integrity. Making untrue excuses for not attending meetings and trainings is another breach of integrity. Slacking off in your personal business building efforts hoping someone you sponsor will do what you are no longer doing is a breach of your integrity. Blaming others for your failures or setbacks is another breach of integrity. It is acting like you have not been taught that failure and setbacks are the two horses you must ride to the finish line. You have been taught that truth. So, blaming and complaining is a form of psychological projection designed to take the spotlight off one's poor performance and shine it instead on some company problem or other people.

The business without problems is the business without opportunity. The people who endured and helped to solve the company's problems on their way to success are now controlling the wealth. Therefore, the winner prepares himself mentally and emotionally to endure and to eventually overcome the obstacles while the losers are unwilling to include and endure the same.

Wisdom is knowing the way things are but not yet the way we wish things to be. Thus, the winner pushes himself on with no retreat from effort until the problems are solved. The losers will pause or completely stop and allow themselves to be emotionally dominated by "what is not yet right." What follows is a loss of enthusiasm for their dreams and a rapid spiral into a caldron of negativity where the only outcome is failure.

## Insight:

Your company will be here, more than likely, as a viable business for many years into the future. Those of us who stay the course now will be compensated well in the future. As with all success if it were easy we would all be riding high with lots of money and personal freedom. The truth is, it isn't easy, but it is ever so achievable for the persevering person with the right attitude.

So, belly up to the challenges that losers will not endure. And, one day you will belly up to a financial banquet feast that the losers will never taste. As always, the advice is offered, but the choice each of us makes will always carry a price.

# *Chapter 41 - 12 Components Of a True Leader*

1. Always display a work-manlike diligence – Become the "plow horse", not the "show horse."
2. Keep working on personal humility and ego control – Study, Read, Model.
3. Become totally resolved to do whatever it takes to make your group and the company great, no matter how big the challenges or conditions of change.
4. Learn to work with the like minded people in your group and your need to manage and motivate is greatly reduced.
5. Set a vision for what you want your team to accomplish and consistently support that vision with focus. Concentrate your effort on the actions required to materialize your vision.
6. Avoid thinking that the "right behaviors" will eventually come from the "wrong people" – Discover the core values of your team leaders – Look for compatibility with the team vision
7. Know the only way to build a team of members who achieve is to make certain they avoid spending time with members who are not motivated and not achieving –avoid energy drainers!
8. Understand that to build a great MLM company, you do not need to simply recruit people, you need to recruit a few great people.

9. Develop unwavering faith amid market changes and difficult business challenges and accept that it might take time but you will find a way to prevail in the end.

10. Don't resist the challenges of change. They have faith that they can adjust and come out stronger in the end.

11. Avoid being "scattered" in your efforts and stay on track! Focus on the necessary "Big Picture" not the matters of little consequence in the long run.

12. Create a "Stop Doing List" and unplug yourself from anything or anybody that is not contributing to or working toward your team vision. Your "Stop Doing List" is often more important than your "To Do List".

# Chapter 42 - Get Serious About Your Business

## Understand Why Competition Is Great!

I write this chapter not to resurrect the already inactive but to encourage the living that still have the capacity to believe in themselves and their future success.

Most people we talk to buy the story of "possibility" for financial independence and true time freedom inherent in the Network Marketing arena, but then most won't do the work required to make it their "personal" success story. It is not difficult to explain why so many people who start never accomplish what they started out to do. All one needs to do is observe their activity level and then listen to their language, which is laden with excuses for non-performance. **Ours is a business of numbers like any other sales business**. The MORE people you expose to the business opportunity and your products or services, the better the odds get stacked in your favor.

Fact! "When you STOP recruiting and selling services, your business **stagnates, dwindles, or dies**. Rather than go out and recruit new people, one begins to look for business growth to come from the people already in their business. Thus one becomes an arm-chair manager of a dying business."

Fact! The best motivator for the people in your business is for them to see you recruiting and helping to build new first level people. Don't philosophize about, "how many first levels can I support?" The good ones don't need a lot of hands on support. They simply plug themselves into all the infrastructure of support from all sources available. All the rest will pretty much "self-declare" their intentions, level of seriousness and staying power within the first 90 days in the business.

You must be accepting of the realities inherent in all business, not just MLM. The shadow of self-doubt lengthens with each passing day for those who are only casually and not seriously involved. This is true of all business. You need to identify the non-serious people in your group quickly, and then adjust your game because you probably won't be very successful at adjusting theirs. You must understand that our business has only three things going on: **It's growing! It's stagnating! Or it's dwindling!**

You must realize that for many people, failure is the path of least "Persistence!" It is their ticket to leave the contest and get away from the self-recrimination that the mirror reflects back to those who half-heartedly do anything in life. Persistence is the key to success in our business.

Remember, failure can never come to the one who falls down, but comes surely to the one who stays down. In our business (yes this business of numbers) you really do fail your way to the top. A vivid awareness and acceptance of this truth will make your journey to success much more palatable as you encounter setbacks, disappointments, and people in your group doing little or nothing. Never let their lack of performance influence your level of performance.

You should be cautious also with the "grumblers" in your group. You will notice they seldom produce much more than anxiety and doubt. They then make a habit of spreading both poisons to the group.

You will also notice that some associates never seem to be able to play the game with the ball they've got. Instead, they are always saying: "If only we had _ _ _ _", "When are they going to _ _ _ _ _?" "Wait till France and Italy opens _ _ _ _." "Gee, somebody's got a lower product price _ _ _ _." Did you read that negative article about _ _ _ _?"

These representatives seem unable to notice that others playing in the same ballpark, and with the very same ball are producing successful businesses. Why? Because their focus is right! Their belief is right! And their work ethic is in full gear! Does that mean that everything is just fine for those who are building successfully? Does it mean they are blind to, or not concerned with the things that need improving? Not at all! They have enough personal motivation and "white hot" desire to persist through or around the problems until they are solved.

The winners in our business know that every successful business has occasional problems, and sometimes even a negative news article. (Which, by the way, is often stimulated by those in direct competition.) In business, just as in life, we usually get what we focus on. The only time we miss the target is when we allow our focus to move off the target.

The winners in our business expect the competition to sometimes be cheaper in their prices but they don't stop selling their own products. Why is it so easy to accept that there are differences in price for almost everything we buy depending on the stores we shop in or the skill or personality of the salesperson? The entire world of commerce is based on competition. Yet we still have thousands of companies producing the very same basic products with varying prices being offered to the buying public.

As a specific market expands, the competition for the customers stiffens and the sedentary life of the large corporations becomes a thing of the past. To keep their customers, they must compete by spending more and more advertising dollars and lowering prices. How far can they go before they suffer big losses due to the high cost of getting and retaining customers? With the large corporations or

stores, there is no personal touch with their customers; just mass media advertising, costly celebrity endorsements, and lower prices to get and retain customers. We don't have the same cost structure. Therefore, if we hang tough, keep on working, and don't belly up, we win.

It's all simple mathematics. There is a financial base line that no company can go below and survive. Our baseline, because of our approach, **"relationship selling, face to face selling,"** is lower than theirs. So stay the course, ride the waves, and endure the storms, for in the end you will be victorious.

It's all a matter of the basic economics of the industry we are in and our unique approach to that industry. Competition is great, especially when you come out on top because of the **"relationship selling" inherent in MLM.**

**Insight:**

"Remember this!  Adversity is easier to endure than an unfulfilled dream.  One offers temporary discomfort, the other a permanent agony over what might have been but never happened." *George Zalucki*

# Chapter 43 - The Truth About Winning And Losing

It absolutely defies logic and sound intelligence for a person to casually gloss over life altering insights and instead continue the "patterns and thoughts" that created their personal conditions of dissatisfaction, failure, and lack of achievement. Yet, that is exactly what people who fail do. Why, one must ask, is this phenomenon so prevalent constantly? The answer is really quite simple. They fail to employ and maintain the needed winning attitudes and behaviors because they know at some deeper introspective level that they are basically fearful of the challenges which they never seemed able to conquer in their past. Add to this the self-observation that: (a) they also really know that they lack the "will" and discipline to stay focused and (b) they also realize they lack a success-worthy work ethic. The combination of this self-awareness, (which is more correctly defined as a brief glimpse of the truth of why they fail) creates anxiety and emotional unrest which most will scramble to relieve and thus they return quickly to the familiar world of excuses and justifications.

Unless this cycle is broken, one is destined to experience a quality of life devoid of the good things life brings to those who do break this cycle. **The truth is . . . nobody is born a success, and nobody is born a failure.** The winners learn from other winners; are influenced by their thoughts and actions; try their best to copy their winning ways, and eventually join them in the winner's circle. The losers learn from other losers; are influenced by their negative self-defeating thoughts and actions and eventually join them in the loser's circle. "Why dream?" they say. "Dreaming is impractical and the work of fools!" "Oh, that motivational psychology and positive thinking is a bunch of bunk!"

STOP . . . I say!  Observe the lives of those who think like this.  Does not their action follow their thoughts and attitudes?  And are not the results they experience in life directly the by-product of those very same thoughts, attitudes and actions?

If you are reading this chapter with an open heart, and mind, combined with a willingness to confront your own truth, it can prove to be life altering for you.  Remember that a mental adjustment always precedes a financial adjustment.  So lets get our minds right so that we can get our finances right.

Ancient wisdom taught over 3000 years ago . . . **"Unless the people dream they perish."**  The implicit, underlying basis for this instruction is clearly that the "Dream" referred to is not an "idle wish" but rather a firm goal or objective to be achieved.  However, if one dreams without faith in the dream's fulfillment, the dream is reduced to just another "idle wish" and therefore can never become a reality.

Dorothea Brande wrote a great book titled "Wake Up and Live".  The entire book was reduced to one of the most powerful success instructions I've ever come across.  **"Act as though it were impossible to fail and you won't fail"**.  Gandhi offered us an equally powerful insight when he explained the role of belief and faith in reaching a goal.  Let me paraphrase, **"If one advances toward a specified objective or goal, and does not lose 'belief' in its attainment; even though they may start their journey without the necessary tools or knowledge of how to get there; if they keep their faith and focus they shall most assuredly obtain the required tools and knowledge along they way."**

After nearly 50 years of working in the field of motivation and achievement psychology, I can attest to the wisdom, truth and power of these insights.

Let me add another truthful insight. **"The road to success is often laden with difficult obstacles."** If there were none to conquer or endure, we'd all be rich and happy.

Let me **restate** here why people fail, so you can learn what NOT to do! You can then decide to do the opposite, which over time, will guarantee your place in the winner's circle.

### Here is why people fail:

1. They lack understanding of what success demands of them.
2. They lack the motivation to learn what is required.
3. They lack the necessary self-discipline.
4. They constantly offer excuses and rationalizations to avoid the uncomfortable aspects of personal growth and change.
5. They lack integrity with self and others.
6. They seem committed to maintaining a poor self-image.
7. They are strongly inclined toward negative thinking and attitudes.
8. They lack self-responsibility.
9. They lack the will to sustain their efforts when disappointments come their way.
10. They have the habit of projecting their failures and shortcomings on others.
11. They have a low tolerance for emotional, physical or financial discomfort.

12. When exposed to the wisdom, instructions and attitudes of the winners in life, they choose instead the influences and thought patterns of the masses who are stuck in lives of quiet desperation devoid of dreams.

Author Robert Anthony in his book titled "Betting on Yourself" (Berkley Books), offers us 10 Positive Assumptions. If you combine his 10 instructions with **"act as though it were impossible to fail"** as Dorothea Brande instructs us, you can start your journey today toward the winner's circle knowing you will get there.

1.  I will make and keep my commitments.
2.  I will find the right people who can help me.
3.  I will look for an answer in every problem.
4.  I will give up "trying" and simply do.
5.  I will make it okay to be wrong and make mistakes.
6.  I will create my own "good luck".
7.  I will not be afraid to lose before I win.
8.  I will do it now!
9.  I will be who I am and become what I was meant to be.
10. I will accept that all things are possible.

**Now you have it.  The rest is up to you!**

**Insight:**
    **"Each one of us chooses the road we will travel, the people we associate with and the thoughts, attitudes and actions we engage in.  Winners simply make different choices than losers.  They think different thoughts, believe different things, adopt different attitudes and therefore produce**

different results in their lives. And that's the truth about winning and losing. And, as always, the choice is uniquely yours..." *George Zalucki*

## *Chapter 44 -Why Missed Awakenings?*

How can one prove or validate life-changing insights to a person who is unconsciously conspiring against accepting them? If the only method of validation is for the person to realize, accept and utilize the offered insights, it is easy to see why most people have great difficulty confronting the behavioral changes mandated by the insights, especially when there is no proof they will work or guarantee success. Teachers, coaches and leaders all wonder in amazement why a person would reject life altering insights especially when the person rejecting them is the very one most often in need of utilizing them. The most often offered explanation is ---"They fear change!"

Let's look a little deeper. Perhaps it would be far more accurate to say it is self-sabotaging, or reluctance based upon one's inner awareness, that to accept the challenge of change is to expose oneself to the possibility of failure and further ego humiliation. Thus, the "thoughts" one has of himself, (self image) is controlling his decision to act or retreat. Unless this cycle of self-limitation is broken, one's life goes on unchanged, remains stagnant, and essentially unfulfilled. The victims of this sad mental saga often go through life with a suspicious eye, unwittingly committed to finding the unworkability or fault with the opportunities being offered to them.

It does not matter that the insights or the opportunity offered could dramatically change the content and quality of their lives for the better. A person needs an adequate level of "self-belief" in order to step out in faith and go for it. This lack of self-belief acts as an "ambition tranquilizer" and a powerful inhibitor of positive expectation.

Some people will disguise their fear of failure by taking the high moral ground. They come across as the custodians of morality and ethics as though they could never engage in or offer another person anything that was not as perfect as **they** think it should be. (In other words, not guaranteed.) These people almost always fail in entrepreneurial endeavors where the life- blood of success is based upon being an integral part of molding the unworkable to eventual workability, the uncertain to certainty and potential for profits into realized profits. This process requires a person to be far more than casually involved. It demands serious commitment.

The nature of human progress in all areas of science or business will clearly show that the progress made was the result of making existing things better and having the guts to be personally involved and passionately engaged in that ongoing process. We humans have always built new progress on the shoulders of what was previously considered as progress, but still needing improvement.

When, for example, a business reaches operational ef- ficiency, and where most growth problems are basically under control, the owner (entrepreneur) only needs an adequate level of "employees" to fill the positions the entrepreneur's hard work and persistence created. The "employee" gets a weekly paycheck and all too often a mental and emotional addiction to the implied, but certainly not guaranteed, financial security offered by the job. The "job" defines its demands and basically eliminates the un- certainty and risk the entrepreneur must face in order to succeed. There is nothing wrong with this approach if it is satisfying to the individual. In fact, statistics will verify that most people take this path for their means of acquiring money because betting on themselves is simply too frightening and risky. However, every choice has a consequence. **So, I ask you, "When is the last time you met a wealthy or financially free person who has worked for someone else?"** If financial freedom is a person's goal in life it is almost 100% certain that they will need to become involved in their own business. If you want to be numbered among the financial elite you will need to think, act and believe like the financial elite. They think possibilities, not limitations! They accept risk as an important component of success! They set specific performance goals and they don't know the word "Quit"!

So, if you want financial freedom, the question and the conclusion are painfully obvious! Is personal change really an option, or is it unmistakably critical? As the great American heavyweight boxing champion, Joe Louis said, "You can run but you can't hide!" It's the same with life-changing insights----you can reject them, but you can never get away from the effects of rejecting them. Remember, in life we harvest what we plant. And all planting begins with "thoughts." Therefore, you must put new thinking into your head before you can expect to get new or different results in your life. This, my friends, is an undeniable law of change. We can elect to run, but the effects of our actions or neglect will always be manifest in our lives.

As I've often said from the platform, "Universal laws don't give a damn if you or I ever learn of them, accept them, or reject them." No, they simply run the game we call life. Wise men know and accept this truth while the unwise persist in their self-imposed delusions where dead dreams abound and mediocrity at best is their companion through life. I have found after 50 years of working in the field of motivational psychology and personal development that the "anticipation" of what change will demand is the biggest deterrent to getting started.

You see, most people do not lack the ability to succeed. What they lack is the willingness to change and endure what is required of them to justify success. I'm convinced that many more people would succeed if they would simply jump in the pool of opportunity with the inner confidence that they will eventually learn how to swim to success if they stay in the pool long enough and keep on stroking. It will never be as tough as our mis-managed imaginations predict it will be. So, step out! Step it up! And, stay the course till you win!

**<u>Insight</u>:**

**Philosopher, Aldous Huxley said it best. "Most ignorance is vincible ignorance. We don't know because we don't want to know!" And, Emerson wrote, "It is impossible for a man to be cheated in life by anyone but himself."**

## *Chapter 45 - Fired Up Or Fizzled Out?*

You can never burn out if you've never been lit up! So let's light up and go! What does "Fired Up" look like?

Paul and Sarah Edwards, Business experts and writers for Entrepreneur Magazine, have studied 107 Successful home-based entrepreneurs since 1989. While these 107 successful entrepreneurs were in different fields and came from all parts of the country and varied widely in age, background and experience, they all had one thing in common. **That one common characteristic was that they all had specific, tightly focused goals! That single-minded focus was the primary reason for their success!**

People who are lukewarm about, or dabble with, their business have never been able to compete successfully with people who are committed to and have fire in their belly for success. You see, it is not possible for your business to take off and grow on its own. It needs to be primed, worked and nurtured over time if you are to succeed. **Consider the following:** What if fate had sentenced you to pursue your business (only on a part-time basis) for 2 years with no option of quitting before then; and that your entire future income for the rest of your life, per month, could never exceed the monthly check you received from your business in the 24th month? Consider now that you are actually confronted with this as a reality. How would you work your business over the next weeks and months right up through the 24th month? The answer you give to this imagined scenario will be very self-revealing.

Let's play with the possibilities. Chances are almost 100% that if this scenario were true, that you would work your buns off to get that month 24 check to the highest level possible. Well guess what is implied here? It means you could succeed if you worked hard enough and with single-minded focus for the next 24 months. On the other hand, being forced with the same scenario, you decided to work the business in a casual unorganized manner. Would you not face a certain disastrous financial future when the 24th month passed? The answer is clearly obvious! You'd be financially devastated for life!

The people who cross the financial independence finish line somehow do whatever it takes to keep their own internal fire burning which, in turn, provides the steam that propels them through the dry seasons of labor, setbacks and disappointments which are inherent in every journey to success. Here's how! They feed on positive inspirational stimulations be they from CD's DVD's, videos, books or other positive people. And, they avoid like the plague the nay–sayers and saboteurs of their success.

Let's face it! If you fail, it won't be because what you were required to do you couldn't do . . . . . . . NO, it will only be because you could have, but you didn't! The failures in our type of business are spawned in a caldron of excuses and projections where the focus shifts from possibilities, to problems to overcome and people to blame. That's not to minimize or make light of authentic glitches or problems we all encounter as we build our business. No. Legitimate concerns need to be addressed and

should be eliminated by corrective action or improved within a reasonable time period.

What you need to guard against, however, is the fact that your own personal shift in mental and physical focus can quickly become the primary reason for your lack of business growth and not the problems themselves.

Have you ever noticed that some people are able to grow their business while including the problems to be sorted? The difference is their faith and belief that the problems will be sorted and the business will become an eventual success.

Have you also noticed that the people who focus their attention predominately on the problems seldom succeed in the business even when the problems are solved? Some say they can't recruit while the problems exist; and then they don't recruit once the problems are removed. Come on now, let's get real here!!

Can you possibly imagine Google, IBM or Microsoft and countless other huge companies arriving at the pinnacles of success they've enjoyed without problems, competition and obstacles to endure, struggle through and eventually overcome? Their will to win and their ability to endure is exactly why they are successful. The same goes for us!

Let's look at professional sports for a vivid example. All pro athletic teams have one goal in mind and it is to win! Each sport uses pre-season training camps as a screening mechanism. The training is rigorous because its primary goal is to eliminate the weak players so that the ones who endure, measure up and are best suited to face the rigors of the upcoming season of competition. In life, whenever we see excellence, be it in business, sports, or science, we see people who endured and overcame many obstacles before they were crowned. What's really different about these people? Andrew Carnegie probably said it best when asked to provide the reasons for his huge business success. He said, **"It's faith; faith in myself, faith in my company and faith in my associates!"**

So here's the lesson! If you combine specific, tightly focused goals with honest and sustained work and then filter both through genuine unwavering faith, you have brewed the guaranteed and age old recipe for success.

So start mixing your own success brew now and I'll meet you on stage as a successful network marketer and we'll both know how we got there!

If you talk to the winners in life, their stories of how each got there are homogenous. And if you talk to the failures in life, their stories and excuses for failure are also homogenous.

## Insight:
**Thomas Carlyle said, "The tragedy of life is not so much what men suffer, but rather what they miss."**

## *Chapter 46 - How To Maintain Positive Expectancy*

 Every worthwhile achievement, in order to be termed worthwhile, implies that it was also "extra-ordinary" and therefore challenging. More to the point----you are going to encounter disappointment with yourself and others; at times self-doubt while at other times frustration and even anger as you work toward your objective.

As you encounter these emotional upsets you will notice they can sometimes come in bunches which can weaken your resolve. When this happens, one of two reactions comes from the individual. The eventual winner will say," It is far better to strengthen my resolve and determination than to diminish my dreams!" However, all those who never get to the finish line have a very different thought process. They say, "I can't take anymore of this stuff!" They conclude it is not worth pushing on and simply give up.

You should also know that most people, when they feel little or no control over their circumstances, would react with disruptive criticism and negative behavior. This is the very reaction that will guarantee their failure.

Remember, emotions and thoughts are inextricably interwoven. Our emotions focus attention and stimulate and shape the nature of our subsequent thoughts. This in turn creates subsequent emotions, then more thoughts and more reactions. If this cycle is negative, and not quickly changed, defeat is certain.

It should be noticed here that there are others, the eventual winners, who are encountering the exact same circumstances, but have a different understanding and interaction with the frustrations inherent in all worthwhile endeavors. They press on! One can only conclude that it is the individual's resolve or lack thereof that determines the outcome.

A closer look at the "survivors" or "winners" reveals some very powerful insights. Every one of them accepted personal responsibility for maintaining positive expectancy and personal motivation. They understood that true sustaining motivation, which compels positive behavior, must be focused on a very specific and highly desired outcome and that their motivation must be inner driven. In order to be inner driven, their motivation needed to be fed constantly with the belief that no matter what the temporary obstacles might be, they would endure, include, overcome, and eventually be victorious. They all, without exception, seemed to realize that countless disappointments, frustrations, oppositions, and intermittent failures always preceded achieving big goals. In other words, they were mentally and emotionally prepared for their journey to success. In so doing, they fortified themselves by associating with positive influences, be they people, books, CD's, or seminars. And, as they did so, their understanding grew, as did their knowledge of people and the processes used by other winners.

**Those who are left in the field of broken dreams never took the fork in the road that said:    Warning...**

**WARNING!** This road is indeed less traveled, but all the winners in life have taken it. You will need to be tough to stay on it for it will test all your strengths and reveal all your weaknesses. If you choose this road, however tough it might initially be, it will guarantee you a new and worthwhile life at the end. Much assistance awaits the willing and committed traveler, but you yourself are responsible for acquiring and using the knowledge you obtain on your journey. You will need to clearly define a worthwhile goal before you start. Small and unclear goals lack the capacity to stir the passions required to endure. Your belief in yourself and your objective must be firm and sustained, otherwise you will quit before you are crowned a winner. You will maintain your positive expectancy only by maintaining your faith and positive influences. Therefore, select your thoughts and associates with care, for they both have the power to lead you to victory or defeat. Take this road only if you sincerely desire to reach your objective. It is not for the lukewarm of heart, the idle dreamer, or the lazy or dishonest person. They will fall by the side of the road and their numbers will be many. Some of them will be your friends or even family members. Do not wallow in pity or self-incrimination at their failure. It was not your thoughts and attitudes that put them there. It was theirs.

**Insight:**

**Remember always that on the highway to success, the further traveled, has hardly any traffic on it! So, travel on my friends! Victory awaits you!**

# *Chapter 47 - Resolutions or Commitments*

The dawn of each New Year brings with it a host of "resolutions" for change or improvement, most of which unfortunately will never be kept. The reason for failure to keep our New Year's resolutions is simply this: "We make them in a state of "emotion" that is temporary and non-sustaining." Our vows to keep them are supported by a will too fragile and weak to persevere when the going gets tough and the emotional climate changes.

Washington University did a study that found that a mere 17% of the people who make New Year's resolutions are successful. So how do we beat the 83% failure rate? First we need to recognize that resolutions without "specific" activity commitments or "activity goals" are nothing more than mere wishful thinking. Don't say, for example, "I'd like to make more money in the year 2010." You need to be very specific! Exactly how much money do you plan to earn and accumulate? Once you know that dollar "specific" back it up by another set of "specifics," namely "specific actions" you must perform and how often in order to reach your goal. Know this! In order for your financial situation to improve, your money-making behaviors have to change or increase and usually both are required. Start by having a serious conversation with the "real" you. No more excuses! You really do know your self-deceptions as they relate to where you are financially. You need to confront those elements in your personality, attitudes, and work habits that need changing. To overpower your past behavior patterns, which have limited your success you need some very powerful incentives that you are committed to obtaining and eventually enjoying. Remember that your bad habits are tied to some reinforcing elements in your life. There is always some struggle to change, so be aware that your mind will at first be gathering thoughts to encourage you to retreat from your resolutions. You will need to get tough with yourself when these thoughts begin and shut them down swiftly. You must take charge of your own mind and direct your thoughts toward your declared objectives.

Become "obsessed" with your goals until you have developed your new habits of thought, emotion, and work. There will be times when you will think "it is not working," or "it's too tough", or "it's not worth it." It is during these tough times that eventual success or sudden failure will be declared. To retreat is certain failure! To persist is eventual victory! To win you must surrender to your goals and in doing so you will have the power to keep going. When adversity hits or your old habits begin to lure you back to mediocrity, comfort, and failure – surrender in this case will be the actual source of your power and will to persevere. A surrendered person is no longer concerned with "resisting" the tough or unpleasant tasks of their mission; they simply include whatever comes and that is the key reason for their success.

You might need help along the way, so listen to motivational CDs and read inspiring books to maintain your resolve. Declare your intentions and goals to a trusted friend or mentor and ask to be kept accountable for producing the required level and nature of the actions necessary to produce success. Your bottom line self-instruction daily is **"Retreat or defeat is NOT an option open to me any longer!"** This time I declare myself the winner!

So let the contest with myself begin! I declare this year to be the best year of my business and personal life. Why? Because I said so - - - and for it to be so, all I need to do is "keep my word" and everything that I need to change or improve will reveal itself to me along my road to success.

I'll close with a quote by Tom Peters, business writer and speaker, **"Obsession doesn't guarantee success. On the other hand, a lack of obsession does guarantee failure."** Every successful and prosperous person will testify to the fact that their lives were out of balance for a short period of time in order to build the financial stage they are dancing on for the rest of their lives.

Why not try what I have suggested in this article for only 90 days. If you do, you will be absolutely convinced that success for you is now just a matter of time.

**<u>Insight:</u>**
**To win you must stop wandering and make a firm decision to see it to the end this time.**

# Chapter 48 - Small Dreams, Little Resolve, No Victory

I am convinced at this time in my life, considering all my experiences, both positive and negative, and considering the lessons I've learned, that success in anything worthwhile takes more persistence, dedication, and action than 95% of the people are willing to provide. All too many people have enveloped themselves in maudlin self-sympathy always looking for the excuses for their shortcomings, perceived disadvantages, and failures.

Their mental focus is really on survival, not prosperity. They settle for average or worse, when excellence and prosperity is an option available to them. They spend their potentially productive hours looking for justification for their lack of financial success.

As time marches on, their self-induced delusions deepen and expand into all areas of their lives. So do the excuses and justifications for failure. They have no real positive vision for their future so they lack the determination required to become successful.

They fail because they quit too soon. They stop doing what is required to win, which is quitting without open declaration. They lose faith when the events and circumstances are against them. They lack the inner strength, which comes only from passionate commitment, to hold on and keep fighting and performing in spite of obstacles, disappointments and episodes of failure. They seem to lack the will to turn temporary defeats and failures into eventual positive victories.

They are more than not weighed down mentally by the negative and find only temporary inspiration when motivated externally. They fail to fully grasp that success is about acquiring the knowledge, skills, behaviors, and attitudes of those who have succeeded before them. Their lives are not experienced as adventures, exploring journeys of self-discovery, but rather as an exercise in survival. They lack a genuine willingness to risk and openness to change. They resist the truth of their limited accomplishments and the true reasons for them.

These people are always looking for circumstances or others to take responsibility for their failures. Their commitment to personal growth and responsibility had a "cut-off date" somewhere in their past and they have failed to reset the clock.

- The only possibility of change for these people is an honest confrontation with themselves.
- No more excuses allowed!
- No more projections of blame on others!
- No more lazy work habits!
- No more crippling fears tolerated!
- No more living without passion and purpose!
- No more resisting what is necessary to do!

## Insight:

I ask you to consider this advice given by Poet Carl Sandburg, "Nothing happens unless first a dream!" To which I add, "It is never too late in life to revise your direction!"

So, re-establish your Dreams! Resolve to see them through! Expect to be victorious!

# Chapter 49 - Eight Principles of Successful Living

To achieve success and fulfillment in virtually any endeavor one wishes to undertake, there is a common set of conditions that must be met. I have found that every great man and woman throughout the pages of history have been a living testament to these prerequisites of achievement, which I call the "Eight Principles of Successful Living."

### Principle #1: A White-Hot Desire

Nothing of any real consequence happens until a person becomes passionate about achieving a specific outcome or objective.

*"Lukewarm desire does not work! Passion stimulates power!"*

Tentative actions stem from tentative thoughts. Both lack the power to self-motivate or influence others. Tentative thoughts produce weak emotions, which create a disappointing outcome or circumstance. People who ultimately achieve their dreams start with - and sustain - a powerful passion for doing so, regardless of the circumstances they meet along the way.

A white-hot desire to have the things you want is matched with equal desire to develop the knowledge and skills necessary to justify having them. Understanding this premise is essential to all achievement. The lack of this understanding is the primary reason for most of our failures.

*Remember:* *Desire breeds Determination, which is expressed in Dedication!*

## Principle #2: Never Wait to "Feel" Motivated

One of the greatest misconceptions about becoming successful is the idea that you should "feel good" or "motivated" before you act. Motivation almost always follows action, but seldom precedes it. As Emerson said: **"Do the thing and you shall have the power."** Champions commit to disciplined actions and pay very little attention to how they feel.

*Remember: Champions don't prime to perform - they perform to prime!*

## Principle #3: Goals Are Essential to Success

A person's power resources are largely invisible. They are housed in the mind and spirit of man. The door to release this power resides in the unconscious mind, but the key to that door is the conscious mind declaring with conviction and accuracy what it wants.

Goals are absolutely indispensable to success. The unconscious mind demands specific intent, or a goal, in order to function as an optimum achievement mechanism. A conquering current always flows with a powerfully declared specific goal.

*Remember: When setting goals, "what I want" will always be equal to "what I don't want to do, struggle with or overcome to get it"!*

## Principle #4: Total Commitment is Paramount to Success

The dynamic expression and ultimate evidence of a person's level of commitment is seen in a constant striving to become exceptional in performance. Thus, actions, not words, are the barometer with which you measure the level of one's commitment. Total commitment also means that you must be able to accept or include whatever obstacles or roadblocks you might encounter along your road to eventual success.

Success, in reality, is seldom a sprint. Success is a marathon. To finish, you cannot be content with mediocrity. True commitment won't allow it.

Laziness and despondency are the saboteurs of commitment. However, the ultimate slayers of your commitment will be the critics you listen to from within ("self-talk") or from without when the going gets tough. Self-doubt, however imposed or accepted, will sap the strength of your commitment. When doubt comes, and it will, you need to abandon your emotions and rely almost entirely on your faith to be greater than your doubt.

*Remember: What one actually does indicates with absolute clarity what one is committed to!*

## Principle #5: Persistence

A determined human spirit is indomitable. Winning in life depends almost entirely on your ability to work hard and persevere. Excitement wears off, but persistence wears down the obstacles between you and success. The price of success is dedication, deprivation, lots of sustained effort - and plenty of doubt and loneliness mixed in to test your resolve. Long hours of preparation are often required to hone the skills and develop the knowledge and techniques that will lead to efficiency and performance and ultimate victory.

To succeed greatly, you must sacrifice greatly. The best way to prepare for the sacrifice is to mentally include it as part of the price. "Surrender to purpose" creates an emotional cushion, which softens the blow of negative emotions associated with disappointments that accompany striving for greatness.

Persistence is "falling in love" with the tedium of constant practice to become better. You have to be willing to do things over and over again. Consistency is the hallmark of all teachers. It is a quality which allows a person of average ability to become a huge success. It is a concentrated patience. It deprives failure the opportunity to become a permanent condition. Most of all, it is the one quality of spirit that transforms a person's dreams into a living, dynamic reality. To become a success at something, you must become a master at it. That takes practice and perseverance.

***Remember: The house of mastery sits at the end of Persistence Street!***

## Principle #6: Set Your Mind to Station WIN

It is absolutely amazing to see how many people today are still not aware of the interwoven relationship between the nature of their thoughts and the conditions in their lives. In spite of the fact that every great spiritual teacher, philosopher, poet and psychologist has taught us about that exact relationship and its significance, most people are still in the dark on this pivotal truth. It is our thoughts that create our motivation to act or not act in any given situation. It is our thoughts about ourselves that determine our capabilities, limitations, "okayness" or "not-okayness," worthiness or unworthiness, lovability or unlovability.

Thus, we think our personal reality into existence. No one else thinks your thoughts but you. No one else is creating your life, as it is perceived by you, except you. Your thoughts are actually creating your experience of life.

It is your thoughts that trigger your emotions of love or hate, happiness or depression, guilt or serenity, and so it goes, on and on. The relationship between your thoughts, feelings and behaviors is reciprocal. You define yourself and your life by the thoughts you think. Everything you experience in your life is experienced in your mind. We are all trapped by our thoughts, our judgments and interpretations of the events in our lives. It is, therefore, essential that we take control of our thoughts.

Success begins in the mind and it is impossible to achieve while your private beliefs and thoughts are hostile to it. Be aware that any thought that serves to diminish you, your strength, your confidence, your intelligence or your security will produce anxiety and stress. You will deal with that stress and anxiety as your thoughts about them dictate. You will either choose to use the stress and anxiety to perform, or you will retreat into resignation which, in turn, must create more thoughts to perpetrate your misfortune. Thus, we become what we think about! "We reap what we sow" is never truer than in the domain of thought.

To change the conditions of your life you must be willing to correct the thinking that created those conditions. This is what Disraeli meant when he said, **"Man is not the creature of circumstances. Circumstances are the creatures of man."** Thoughts, themselves unseen, nonetheless work their effects unerringly. Consequently, you receive what you think about most of the time.

Reveal your dominant thoughts and a person who understands this concept can write an accurate description of your life. Our lives as they are, therefore, are a perfect advertisement of our dominant thoughts. There is a constant creating dialogue between our thoughts and our conditions in life. Change the thoughts, and you eventually change the conditions.

This truth must be too simple to grasp, for too many people never catch on. The works of Dr. William James says it best: **"You can alter the conditions of your life by altering your attitudes of mind!"**

*Remember: You may not always control what happens in your life, but you have absolute control over what you decide to think about what happens. Take control of your thoughts and you take control of your life!*

## Principle #7: Have an Upbeat Vibration As You Work and Live

Enthusiasm is the least expensive yet most effective cosmetic in the world. It is beauty dancing for its own enjoyment. It is the fuel that propels great actions. It is an unequaled attention-getter. It is life's primary expression of appreciation of itself. When combined with sincerity, it is the most enduring of all positive personality traits. It compels us to look for the best in all situations. It makes you a human magnet, pulling close the people and circumstances you need to be involved with to reach your goals. It will transform a sincere wish into a vivid reality. You discover your real self and your talents when you are enthusiastic. As an added bonus, you feel truly alive.

Being "laid back" may be considered a cool attitude in some circles, but the people who get what they want in life are expressive and alive in their actions. They abandon pretense and get flat-out excited about what they are doing.

True self-expression flows from an enthusiastic spirit. When you are really fired up for the task at hand, you discover who you really are and what your powers to create can actually achieve. In the final analysis, there are only two types of people on the planet: Those who are inspired and those who are not! Uninspired people get what is easily available and not very satisfying.

*Remember: Enthusiasm is an art. It must become a learned attitude, totally independent of favorable or unfavorable stimuli.*

### Principle #8: Live Life Now
The achievement resources we have, as humans are awesome powers when developed and directed toward specific objectives. The weaving, connecting and maturing influence is TIME. When understood as a limited resource wherein the virtually unlimited resources of our minds express themselves, it becomes crucial to develop a healthy relationship with time. Most people, since they are not specific with their intent, have a neurotic preoccupation with time and its apparent limitations. They are likely to squander it or struggle with not having enough of the stuff to accomplish what needs doing.

The crucial element of time is clearly its use. This is one area where we all unquestionably are created equal. We all get the same amount for doing the deeds of a day. How does one allocate time, and on what activities does one spend or invest it?

Time in this context becomes a critical factor in achievement. Choice becomes of critical import, as well.

When one chooses to do a particular thing, it requires time. That single choice eliminates all other choices for a specified number of minutes, hours, or days. Now it becomes clear that time is a limited, and therefore, precious resource, which should be invested very wisely.

Would I put my money (resource) in a bank that paid no interest, or in a bond that had no history of positive performance? No! Why? Because it would be an unwise investment. Yet I will seldom audit my use of time, my most precious commodity - my life expressing itself in the context of a limitation. Wow! I need to wake up!

Life is a NOW experience and if I am to be blessed to be here tomorrow, all I'll have is another NOW to make it happen.

In conclusion, life is about growth, about "becoming," within a limited period of linear time called Earth life. If life is to have meaning, it must have purpose. Purpose on this planet is manifest in the context of time. Becoming all you can be, given your unique self, is the ultimate joy life offers. The journey is recorded in time. Its wise use is all you and I have with which to "become" our purpose.

This is a universe of laws and operating principles. Learning comes through concentrated study. Mastery, however, comes through tedious repetition of the principles and rules of the game you are playing. The game you're playing is LIFE, and every day is Super Bowl Sunday!

***Remember:  Life is the ride and Time is the train.  Make the most of your trip and become all you can possibly become on your journey!***

# *Chapter 50 - Songs To Encourage You!*

**The following are two songs I sang on a CD album I recorded with the famous Muscle Shoals Recording Studios in 1996.
The lyrics apply so well to the Network Marketers journey.**

## Never Say Its Over!!

To have a vision and a dream
To be the best that you can be
To have a heart that can believe
In what only you can see
When you feel the wind of change
And you have to face the rain
There's a reason for the storm
It comes to make you stronger
Stronger than before
So, never say it's over
Till the race is through
Got to keep the dream alive
'till you cross the finish line
So, never say it's over
And, you'll see the champion in you!
You can change reality
You can find your destiny
Have the strength to carry on
When all your hope is gone
Then your faith will pull you through
Make a winner out of you
There's no mountain you can't climb
Success is waiting for you
On the other side
So, never say it's over
Till the race is through
Got to keep the dream alive
'till you cross the finish line
So, never say it's over
And, you'll see the champion in you!

### <u>Keep Your Eyes On The Rainbow!</u>

Take life and live it
Take love and give it
Do what's right and
you just can't go wrong
Take time and share it
Take heart and bear it
Take a chance before

The chance is gone
You only live once
No, it don't come back around
Might as well live it up
It sure beats livin' it down
If you think I'm crazy
I'm proud to be insane
But, if you keep your eyes on the rainbow
You won't mind the rain
Be good and know it
Be true and show it
Take enough and leave too much alone
Be a light and shine it
So the lost can find it
Be a mountain not just a rolling stone
You only live once
No, it don't come back around
Might as well live it up
It sure beats livin' it down
If you think I'm crazy
I'm proud to be insane
But, if you keep your eyes on the rainbow
You won't mind the rain

# Section 5 – The Summary

# *Profile Of A Champion*

## *A Personal Conversation With George*

The "Profile of a Champion" is really the summary of all the things I think one needs to incorporate in their life in order to live a fulfilling and happy life. I am thoroughly convinced life works when you and I are contributing our talents, not only to the benefit of ourselves, but also for the benefit of all humanity. I have spent a good deal of my life looking at what I would call the "cluster traits" - the "components" that seem to fit together to build a championship life. And I'd like to tell you rather directly, if you'll permit me, rather emphatically, what it is that you need to be developing and employing in order to become a Champion.

**The things that I'm going to discuss with you do not belong etched on a pad.** They belong etched and rooted in the fiber of your being. They should in fact become the basis upon which you go out and challenge life from your particular vantage point. For if these things do not become a part of you, there is very little chance that you will make your mark. You should also notice that I challenge the illusion that others are greater than you. There are many flowers in the garden. Each and every one contains its own beauty and expression. You need to accept yourself like that. Soon you'll discover that you can chart the course of your own destiny if you are willing to do the work to put the basic ingredients of what it takes to win in place. It should also be clear to you that winning for the Champion is not at the expense of someone else loosing their dignity or feeling 'less than' because he or she crossed the Champion's path. All winning should be based on fair play and integrity. We also need to recognize that we truly live in a world of abundance. Shortage is an illusion. What we lack is the proper level of motivation and internal strength to shape our life the way we want it. We act confused about what it will take to make a success in my life. What should I be thinking? What should I be attempting to acquire? How do I develop myself so I can increase my potential as I go from day to day?

I have found that the starting point, there is not even a close second, is the recognition of your personal dignity and uniqueness as a human being. When you were born, you overcame incredible odds to be here. You could have been millions and millions of other human beings when you consider the possibilities of genetic combinations. YOU uniquely survived the greatest war in the history of humanity - the biological war to be alive in the first place. Was not nature speaking in her own subtle voice when she gave you the gift of life? Was she not in agreement with your desire to express yourself and be alive?

If you do not take responsibility for being alive, if you do not take responsibility for developing the gifts that you have, if you do not take responsibility for contributing to the rest of humanity, in each of these areas, to the degree you don't take responsibility - to that very degree, you shall trade off the quality of your life. To think it is otherwise would not be true. Why is it that so many live with the illusion that it is difficult to take responsibility for their life and create it the way they would really like it to be?

When you were born, you knew your own magnificence. You didn't hate anybody. You had no judgments against anybody including yourself. You lived as though you had magical powers. Everything you touched was at your disposal to bring joy and delight to you. As a child, you fumbled and often fell, but you challenged life with an open spirit. And, it was all so natural. But, for most of us, we grew up and lost the spirit of our childhood. Jesus said, **"Unless ye become like children you shall not inherit the kingdom"**. It is such a powerful instruction. What are children like? What did we lose by our desire to be secure and avoid the challenges that would draw the best from us? Why did we trade off that innocence of childhood, that challenging spirit that we had, to go forth and shape our life, to adventure forth? What died in us? And if we can recognize it, can we resurrect it? If I did not think it were so, I would not do this work. I have seen people that have chosen to re-awake in a moment of insight and have chosen never to go to sleep again. You see, each of us have had many teachers. Each of us have been privileged to have other human beings that have tried to influence us in a positive way; those that lived their lives with a passion to pass their knowledge on to us with wisdom that would have served us well. It's time that we began to listen anew.

 Nothing happens unless first there is the motivation to do, have, or accomplish something specific. The key is <u>DESIRE</u>. I want to be different. I want to get in touch with this power. I want to have my life work better than it's working now. So the beginning point of all achievement - the impetus that you need to have first and foremost is a **WHITE HOT DESIRE** to become more or have more than you presently possess.

Be mindful, however, that **LUKE WARM** will not work. **"The universe", as Socrates said, "does not favor the timid". "Tentative" has no power.** Being tentative is an expression of weakness. It is an invalidation of your innate power. It's telling 'Source', your creator and your true nature; "I don't have what you gave me". It's a denial of the truth. There is not a person in this world that cannot become more than they've become thus far. Is that not true?

So, I need a passionate desire to make a difference in my life. You see folks, meeting our needs does not provide enough impetus; it does not have enough fuel; it does not have enough power, to bring forth our greatness. Meeting our needs is simply a logical consequence of "being alive". We need to be willing to passionately reach beyond our comfortable grasp day after day after day. Not with the mindset of "struggle and effort" but with a surrender to our defined purpose, realizing what this type of thinking can bring to you, your family and the rest of humanity. I desire to be better. That's what I want. Don't let go of that desire. Feed it every single day! Listen to inspirational tapes! Read inspirational books! Turn off that TV or find programs that nurture these qualities in you. We can clearly see every day the result of people not working toward the championship life and the impact that this lack of inspiration has on the quality of their lives. "Well, I'm going to change". When? Now! Now! You see our relationship with time is terrible. "When I get around to it I'm going to read some good books." "When it's convenient for me I'll start on personal improvement". You must honestly become aware of the stories you tell yourself and then take responsibility for the results that are now your life. I will tell you clearly, no one sits independent or apart from being at cause in his or her life. In other words, what you have in your life today is a consequence of what you have been in your life up to this day. If you don't have it the way you want it, wouldn't it suggest you need to do something different? My definition of insanity is pretty simple, "doing the same things you're doing day in and day out and expecting different results". We don't stop to think about these things that can transform our lives. No, instead, we do things routinely! We don't want to stretch out and face and confront all those emotions that stop us. And yet we say, "we want". The observation I have made with most people is that their desire to have things greatly exceeds their desire to do the things that would justify getting those things they say they want. Why don't we tell the truth? We want, but we don't want to do what it is that can bring us what we want. Did you ever notice the struggle of your will? It's incredible! "I'd like to be thin and I love apple pie". "I'd love to be in shape but I hate to exercise". "I'd love to be intelligent but I hate to read or study". Tell the truth. Do you really work on personal improvement or do you simply react to life's conditions and say, "Well, I'm doing the best that I can," marching with the mass of humanity at 90 miles an hour to nowhere specific. Are you willing to be different? Are you really willing to be different and face the ridicule that might come along with declaring a new life for yourself?

When you declare that you're awake and that you are going to make a difference in your life, be prepared for the "scoffers". Be prepared for those people who can't stand your new reflection in their own lives. No longer allow anyone to invalidate your dream once you begin to dream again. They have no right to take it from you unless you throw it in their arms and abandon it.

"Live with passion" is what I'm suggesting! Passion your way; but with clear intention; a defined expectation of a result with integrity and full commitment. Have a plan.

For it should be clear to you by now that if you don't know what you want, anything that comes will have to do. And if you don't know what it is you want, how do you know you don't already have it? "I want to be rich," says the man. And I say to the man, "No, concern yourself first with becoming a person of value and riches will be added to you". "I want to be bright and smart," says the man. I say, "no, concern yourself first with study, dedication, and discipline and then knowledge will be the by-product or the consequences". "I don't have much in my life," says the man. And I say, "Look honestly, have you given much in life?" And the answer will inevitably be "no I haven't" followed by "but I did the best I could." Never is that statement true because you have more going for you than you've ever put in the game. I'm clear about that. People in emergencies demonstrate it over and over and over again. People who passionately love people see them in jeopardy do super human things by normal standards. So we're back to the trap of the mind, aren't we, thinking thoughts of limitation and survival? Desire is number one. And, if it is lacking, we don't stand a chance of ever going beyond a life of basic survival.

Now, we have to look at how we make choices. What makes me decide? Is it my sense of myself, my ideas about the player in the game of life - i.e., me and my self-image? Yes! To win you must re-create your self-image. You need to clearly get off the past- you are not your past. **You are now and forever more the arranger of the events now and in your future**. All past events are gone forever! It is sad to see so many people live the present moment with incredible concern for their past, thematically reconstructing the past as though it didn't happen or, thinking "if I did it this way" or "if I had done it that way", maybe it would be different now. We waste enormous amounts of "now" time when we belittle ourselves to the point where we invalidate our capabilities, by wallowing in past mistakes. We need to consider how one might clean that up. Most of us have gotten our impressions of our limited capabilities as we were growing up. We developed a poor self-image. However, many of us found that it was a comfortable place to hang out. It became our excuse for not really swinging the bat at life. "Oh, I can't do this or that". How hard did you try? How much of you were really in the game or did you simply "sell out" because some authority figure told you, "You couldn't do it". The world is full of people who just didn't buy into limited self-appraisal and performed incredible feats and overcame incredible obstacles. How you view your capabilities and personal power determines the limits of and the size of your dreams.    To correct the self-image, we need to become incredibly truthful with ourselves. If I were to look at the central cause of most personal problems: it's our lack of integrity within ourselves and with others. One would say in a modern world, "Integrity, huh, you must be a fool". And look at the world we have from the corporate boardroom to the hallowed halls of government, to the smallest structures in society.  We have all but forgotten the necessity and power of integrity. Do you think that you and I are not responsible as well?  We are, because we tolerate this lack of integrity at some level in our own dealings. The truth is, we have an obligation to be honest with each other. We have an obligation to be honest in our business dealings. I believe at some level we are all aware that anything less than honest dealings with others will sooner or later reflect back to us in a negative way. We lose friends! We lose money! We lose credibility! We gain only a bad reputation, anxiety, worry, uncertainty, and eventually failure.

You must understand that it is the lock that determines the key - not the key that determines the lock. This is an intelligent universe with laws.    These laws pay no heed to our personal opinions about their existence. They just are! The laws of this universe are interconnected and absolute. It's as if I had something behind my back that you could not see, I say to you nonetheless, "it is there independent of your vision". You may have an opinion as to whether or not it exists but I want you to know it exists independent of whether you agree or disagree. That is the way of the laws of this universe. Some are the laws of your forefathers. Some are the laws of your religious beliefs. Their controlling power exists independent of what you and I may want to think about them. And if they are true and you violate them, who are you ultimately violating, if not yourself? You see, it always comes back to us. We're always back to the operative center; it's you and I. We're it! We're it! That's life! You were born "It", and all too many spend most of their lives looking for excuses to explain their lack in life. "I don't want to be responsible for everything in my life". "That looks like too much effort". "Don't let me tell the truth. If I tell the truth what will happen?" "Why be truthful in my business dealings, when so many others are not? What shallow thinking! It takes real character to rise above the shallow standards accepted by most as being okay.

Are you ready to stand-alone so that others can see you and begin to follow? I assert that the future of humanity rests on a renewed commitment to integrity. If I want to think well of myself, I need to tell the truth about my God-given talents, those I have, but failed to develop. I'm going to tell you how to start telling the truth. We're going to stop hiding out in life. We're going to re-discover who we are and we're going to re-discover the potential we have. It's going to become a personal mission. We're not going to 'half play' at this because when you 'half play' you lose. You need to play 'full out' in life to win. I've never met a winner who held back. Just think of the ludicrous reasons we give for holding back. "I don't want to look stupid". "I don't want to feel embarrassed". "I don't want to feel incompetent". "It looks like a lot of work". Just look at the reasons we give for not having a full life. It's really kind of disgusting, isn't it? But, if our mind does not start observing these controlling excuses, we're not going to dissipate their power over us. It's not going to happen - because as your mind constructed them, so too your mind must destroy them.

So how do I improve my self-image? I need to start doing some new things so I can start believing some new things about myself. The self image is tied to the belief system, i.e., the thoughts about myself. "I think I'm capable - I think I'm incapable". "I think I'm ugly - I think I'm handsome". Notice you inner talk about your self-image. If you want to know how unaccepting you are of yourself tonight, go home, take off all of your clothes in the privacy of your bathroom and, do a slow observing 360 degree rotisserie in front of the mirror and see how much you admire, or how much you disparagingly comment inwardly about how you look. You will notice your self-declared deficiencies 10 times the ratio that you will notice the attractive qualities of yourself. What is it about us that we are so disparaging toward ourselves? Folks, you're the only player in your game. Be nice to you. You're the horse in the race. Take care of you. Think well of yourself. For we know clearly today that a child without self esteem, without self-confidence, barely stands a chance at success in life unless he or she gets help with re-constructing their self image. Who are we if not children with a few added years on us? Loose the shackles of your self-limiting thoughts and live everyday as though everyday is "Super Bowl Sunday"!

Will it be uncomfortable to do new things? It will be uncomfortable to the degree that you resist what needs to be done. I am reminded of the time I was working with a young man who was terrified to speak. But, after personal coaching, he confronted and **<u>included</u>** that fear. Now he has spoken often in front of large groups and continues because the power of that confrontation dissipated that which was his self made ghost, a restraining ghost of his own making. You need to identify those ghosts in your own life. You need to know that you are in fact a channel of incredible power. How much of the power do you want? Start being a mental plumber. Remove the mental and emotional sludge. Start opening the valves of resistance to life's cry to express itself through you. Allow yourself the openness of possibility and play. Enjoy! Enjoy the journey. **The trip around the world is never about the destination. It's about the trip.** Enjoy each day, fully participating. There's no tomorrow! It's a fabrication of anxious anticipation! There's no such thing! And

there's no yesterday that can do you any good today. There is **NOW**. So **now** I'm going to improve my self-image. I'm going to start venturing out **now**. Get yourself a coach. Get someone that you trust. Ask them to encourage you to do something that you know will help you grow. Get a support system in place. If it's a spouse or a friend, team up together. There is such synergy when two people are working

together to confront their fears. Get that extra encouragement. Start listening to inspirational tapes. Listen to the words and read about the lives of people who overcame incredible obstacles. For they are you, out of the chair and in the game. That's what you have to recognize. They are not different. They only think and act differently. No creator of a loving nature would have dealt you a deck that you could not have played successfully one way or another. But we compare, don't we? We compare all the time. We say, "I'm not this - I'm not that - if I were this - if I were that - if I were only - if I were this - if I were that." Stop the comparing! Just accept that you are unique, special, and powerful. So, perhaps it is time to recognize this truth and get on with the work and joy of proving it to yourself.

Do I need goals once I start feeling better about myself? Oh, you bet. Your goals will create the vacuum - the inertia that pulls you out of comfort, which, in turn, compels you to stretch out and reach for your target. It's in the "stretching" that I begin to conquer. Now watch what is happening. As I conquer the little steps, my self-confidence has a solid new belief basis in-fact to start thinking differently of myself. Little steps accumulated over time and I gain more power. I'm now validating my new power. Another step, more power. All of a sudden I see the results of my improvement. Six months ago I was fearful to take the first step. Now I look at the peak of the mountain and it's attainable. It's in reach because I began - I took the first step and then I took the second. I now realize that there are very few paths that go straight to a worthy accomplishment. You need to be willing to include and accept that the detours are necessary for your growth. The stumbling blocks are placed in your path so that the lessons you need to learn are learned, also so you can appreciate and treat your eventual success with dignity and well-deserved pride. So I've decided I'm going to go out there and do some new things. If you want to know what it is you need to do, ask someone you trust who loves you. And say, "I don't care what you say. I know you love me." "Tell me what would serve my growth" and be willing to listen. You would be amazed when someone truly loves you the advice they could give you. It doesn't come from their selfishness. It comes from their wanting to see you become all you can become. You will discover that you can do things you thought you could not do. You've now opened up the Pandora's box of your power.

You will begin to notice that the challenges of life are uniquely different than they were before you started. "I need to set goals". Why? Because the human mind is structured in such a way that unless it is given a clearly defined objective it lacks direction and it wanders aimlessly. Any outcome will do! Any job will do! Why? "Because I need a job so that I can make a living". Hear your self-talk. It's saying, "I want to survive so I'll take anything" and then I'll complain. "No, I need a clearly defined objective". I need to point the arrow of my intentions clearly at a target. Why? Because without it, I start to play games. Don't you? There will never be a sense of urgency or a compelling energy until you are committed to performing something specific. Now, I'm going to give you a great secret of achievement. I found this to be an attitudinal common denominator in all-great achievers. And it's a paradox of sorts. It goes like this: Once it is, I know what it is I definitely want, (a) I declare it as my birth-right to get it and (b) immediately after that "I surrender to my objective!" **I surrender to my purpose!** A non-surrendered person encounters obstacles with a sense of resistance and annoyance. They feel it's not okay for obstacles to be there and they quit when the going gets tough. Obstacles and challenges make them feel uncomfortable and incompetent, so they get out of the game. But when I'm surrendered to an objective, I automatically emotionally include what's there. "Oh, this episode is failure? Yes, I understand. But that doesn't make me a failure. That's an occurrence of failure". Could I have done or learned more that would have prevented the failure? Tell the truth! Was I really competent and prepared when I came at this challenge? Or, was I lazy in my preparation. Tell the truth! And all you will find if you come from truth is that you will automatically put in the corrections in your life that point you toward abundance. That's what it means, "to flow with the river" on the river's terms, not on your terms, not on my terms

Now comes rejection. Rejection experienced in the past used to paralyze me. It would make me say, "I can't stand that feeling so I'm not going to participate!" I begin to walk around like a defense mechanism; analyzing where rejection might come from, and with my mismanaged imagination, I can make it come from almost anywhere. I will not participate in the opportunities and challenges of life because I fear being rejected. But now I'm surrendered to my objective, and in that surrender I'm no longer resisting rejection. The mere fact that I stopped resisting it means I won't have the same emotional affliction that I would have if I were still resisting. In many aged philosophies, the idea and notion of resistance being connected to pain is very vivid in their understanding of reality. It's only here in the Western world that we keep resisting everything emotionally unpleasant, that we create and compound our anguish.

Now if my mind says, "This is going to be mighty tough", I want you to remember, "Your thoughts attract the conditions of your life and your thoughts are: "This is going to be tough". How do I vibrate now as I encounter the world? I begin looking for evidence of my thought, and then when it shows up I say, "See, I told you so. It was tough!" not recognizing you created "tough" from your own prior conclusion, "It's going to be tough!" But if I say with power and conviction, "That's what I want." I am absolutely committed to getting it, and I truly expect to get. The outcome is only a matter of time.

I then only need to ask myself a couple of questions. You might however resist these, so let's get right down to the nitty gritty. I know what it is I want. I said what it is I want. I declared what I want.

Question No. 1 - "Is what I'm about to do now, moment by moment by moment, is it leading me toward my objective or away from my objective and tell the truth." You'd be amazed at how much editing you're going to have to do about what you speak you want and how inconsistent your behavior is to support your spoken intention.

Question No. 2 - we should want what we desire to be satisfying and worthwhile. We don't want it to be a harmful to others. So now, Question No. 2 - "Is the decision for action I'm about to make going to intentionally harm another person?" And if the answer is no, proceed with full vigor. If the answer is yes, start again, rethink, and take a different course of action. The temptation will often be expediency. "I don't have enough time". "Everyone is doing it that way". "It's not such a big deal". Over time a little bit of tolerance and bending of ethics will become a whole lot more and pretty soon we have blurred right from wrong.

But if the principles and guidelines for a good life are what they are, and, if this universe comes from intelligence, then I've got news for you. It's a universe of laws and you and I are subject to them regardless of what we believe. We have the capability to think, and the capability to choose, and the capability to love and to hate, and the consequence of our choices are the conditions we eventually find ourselves in. Therefore be wise in your choices of thought and of selecting friends and associates.

 Now, back to goals. A goal has two equal sides that act like a scale weighing gold. On one side is what I want. But, understand this! On the other side is what I don't want to do or put up with to get what I say I want. So, if you dream lofty dreams, what must you be prepared for? Many things that the mind will convince you are unbeatable obstacles. So, if you dream lofty dreams be prepared for obstacles equal to the value of the accomplished dreams.

You say you want opportunity. Let me describe it for you. Opportunity is a coin with two faces. On one side is opportunity equal to its face value. On the other side of that same coin are obstacles equal to the face value of the same coin. So, if I have a great opportunity what will be inherent in that great opportunity - a few obstacles - or many? So if you're dreaming lofty dreams what must you be prepared to include? There will be many obstacles for you to overcome. There's never been a worthy victory without a struggle.

What does all this mean? The truth is you're not going to

accomplish big things without first working on you. You're the one that needs to be worked on. The pursuer of opportunity is you. The better you get, the better your efforts will produce desirable results. Can you see the undisputable connection here? The truth is and always has been that you are the one who is responsible for the outcome. That being said, a truth-revealing question follows. Are you striving daily for more self-competency? As you grow, just like the analogy of the scale, your accomplishments will equally grow. Are you developing your skills or are you like most simply wishing for things to get better and doing little or nothing to self-improve? If you want to succeed, you must separate your thinking, attitudes, and behavior from the masses of idle dreamers; always "intending" but mostly "pretending".

Each of us has the power of choice and each choice is a step toward some future outcome. There is no escaping this truth. Your life as it exists today is a manifestation of your accumulated thoughts, emotions, attitudes, and the choices made by you over time. For example, if learning was unimportant for you, notice the relationship to where you are economically as a result of that choice. If you complain about your circumstances, or blame others for it, notice the quality of your life as a consequence. If you lack self-motivation, notice the many good things that you and your family will never enjoy. As the great prize fighter, Joe Louis once said, "You can run, but you can not hide." To which I add, "You can avoid the truth, but never its justice"

The developmental steps of the champion begin with awareness, focus, and then proceed on with commitment and persistence until a specific objective is achieved. So, now that I have learned the truth of achievement and the absolute necessity of commitment, I declare, "I want to be committed and I need to be committed to my objective". What is commitment? I'll tell you what it is. Commitment is doing the thing you said you would do long after the mood you said it in has left you. For most people, commitment is "I'll do what it takes - whatever it takes - for as long as it takes - until (and the list is endless), until it's uncomfortable, until it doesn't fit my picture - until it gets too tough, until I get ridiculed or frustrated, until, until." The list of "untils" eventually flush the dream.

You must also be vividly aware that commitment is tied directly to persistence, which is tied to the next quality I want to discuss. If I were to send you out to research one word, and then, tie that word to the lives of the great achievers of history, no matter where they came from, this one word would be PERSISTENCE. You would get a vivid awareness of the necessity to hang in when your mind tells you not to. You need to be aware that the mind wants to create an escape hatch from your resolve when the going gets tough. You do know that don't you? The mind will talk you into starting, and the mind will talk you into giving up. But, as we've learned surrender includes the mind keeping its commitment. You see the mind must keep your commitment, if you hang tough and do not allow it any justifying thoughts or excuses to reverse your commitment.

**COMMITMENT IS WHAT TRANSFORMS A PROMISE INTO A REALITY.** It is you keeping your integrity with what it is you said you were going to accomplish. Why are you going to accomplish it? For one reason and only one reason - because you said you would. All other reasons are going to fail you sooner or later. So, become your word. Do what you speak. That's real power. Commit to it and tie into the power of persistence. Shakespeare said, **"Much rain wears the marble."** Og Mandino said, **"I shall persist**

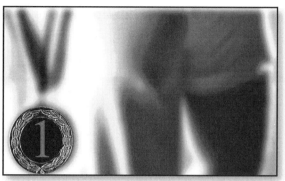

**until I succeed."** Listen to that talk. Where is the escape door in that talk? **"I shall persist until I succeed."** You are left with no way out. That is the self-talk of a winner. Conversely, the self-talk of a loser is, "I will do what it takes as long as it's not too tough". As long as the goal looks as though it's within ready grasp and everybody agrees with me, then I'll stay in the game. That's the language of everybody who falls short in life. Perhaps we fail because Nature knows we have power. And Nature can't tolerate our self-deceptions. Nature or should I say life dishes back to us the conditions of our life in direct proportion to how we develop ourselves to compete in the marketplace of life's countless opportunities. The closer you look at the accomplishments of a champion; you will see a direct correlation between deserving to win and winning. Common sense tells us that we must put money in the bank before we can draw money out of the bank. Doesn't it make sense to you that one must put forth before one can ask to receive or expect to receive? Do you live by that philosophy, as opposed to "what's in it for me?" People with the latter philosophy stopped growing as a person a long time ago and then became a reactor to life instead of a creator of life. Is that not true for many of us when we tell the truth; until we wake up to reality? In varying degrees, we are all convicted by that observation. The art of correction is first acknowledgment, then acceptance of truth, followed by a firm resolve to be committed to paying the dues required to justify success.

Persistence is awesome! It's absolutely awesome! **PERSISTENCE IS WHAT TAKES AN ORDINARY PERSON OF ORDINARY TALENT AND MOLDS THEM INTO A CHAMPION**. Persistence! If you hang in long enough you're going to get good at what you need to do. You know it and I know it. But if it doesn't flow easy, what's the temptation? "Eh - I'm not cut out for this". And then we go and repeat the same self-deluding cycle some place else. Have you noticed? To become a champion, there comes a "Red Sea" place where we need to take a stand. We need to take a stand with ourselves and recognize that we need to 'hang in'. We need to do what it is we say we are going to do and recognize clearly that persistence is the wings upon which the glory of victory rides in all areas of life.

What else is persistence? **PERSISTENCE IS CLEAR DYNAMIC EVIDENCE OF YOUR FAITH IN YOURSELF AND YOUR PROJECT.** Persistence is tied directly to Faith. Remember the power of the mind? The power of the mind was tied directly to Faith; faith in yourself, faith in your objective, and faith in the capabilities that you have. Persistence is tied to faith and faith is evidence that my commitment is unwavering.

Next, let us discuss the power of Enthusiasm. To me enthusiasm demonstrates one's appreciation of being alive and involved. People show enthusiasm in different ways. It's an outward expression of one's inner vibrations. Be enthusiastic your way. The clearest evidence of enthusiasm is openness to life's opportunities and challenges. The enthusiastic person never looks for the hole in the donut. They look for the solutions when problems arrive. They look for ways they can contribute. So, be enthusiastic! Want to know why? It works! Studies done on sales groups indicate the reasons people buy their products. 51% of the persuasion to buy was related to the enthusiasm of the sales person. What is sales, if not transference of a conviction from a seller to a buyer? Enthusiasm demonstrates "I believe." Can you see the connection? It's hard to be enthusiastic if your belief is not there. There are going to be times when you will not feel enthusiastic. We talked about that earlier. But, what did we learn about emotions? If I start my endeavor with the intention of being enthusiastic about what I'm doing, very shortly in the action of doing, I begin to experience the emotion that I did not have when I began. But if I wait for that desired emotion, I may wait a long time before it emerges as a power source for me to move into action. If I wait, I'm relying on being "fired up" as being necessary for action. SUCCESS DEMANDS A DISCIPLINE OF ACTION. Folks, listen to me. Success follows sustained actions performed over time. You just want to progress a little bit forward each day. What's the big mystery? Why don't we try it? Why don't we really finish what we start out to accomplish? Follow these insights. I can guarantee you this. Employ them for a year and there is no way that your life will be the same, absolutely impossible that it will be the same. You will have things in your life that you were dreaming about. You'll have people in your life that you want to be with because you are enthusiastic and committed. When you go out, don't go and look for the person you want, BECOME THE PERSON YOU WANT and you will find that person you were looking for was looking for you. First, you become. We're back to the mirror. The only place that one's life improves is in the mirror, with integrity. No more excuses.  No more blaming.  No more, somebody else did something to me.  Today is the end of that game. And if you mean it, you will be amazed what is going to happen for you. You'll write me a letter or you'll see me some other time and say "I couldn't believe there was so much magic in just plane truth and common sense."   Yes, there is magic in awareness.  Get off everybody else's case including your own and just start to live each day with direction, intention and passion.

As we come to the end of this book, I couldn't close without

talking to you about what I consider to be the greatest power in the universe, **LOVE.**   We need a whole lot more of it.  Love to me is the healing balm of every injustice and it always works for the good and benefit of humanity. And it's opposite, Hate, I see as the great destroyer of lives.  Love is boundless.  There is no limit.  Absolutely no upper limit.   You and I can be open to love day in and day out to the degree that we want love if we will give up our judgments and assessments and just be and let be.  Love in your family relationships - powerful stuff.  Love of your neighbor - powerful stuff.  Love of the world you're in - powerful stuff.  So what is life about?  Life is about you, life is about me, and life is about us.  We are not really different.  I know how you feel when you feel bad.  I think you know how I feel when I feel bad.  I think I know how you feel when you're not in integrity because I know how I feel when I'm not.  I think I know how you feel when you're happy because I know how I feel when I'm happy.  I think it's great when you can smile because I've been with you, and I think it's great that I can smile because you've been with me. Whether it's at work, with your neighbors, together with your families, love works. Go for it! There is no way the cup of love is ever full.

So, when are we going to start all this? When? Right now! Time! Time! I think that time is an invention of the universe so that all events in the universe won't happen simultaneously and we'd be confused. You see, life is the present moment. End of story. Let me say it again. Life is nothing more than the present eternal moment you are in right  now, nothing more. Let me say it again. Your life is a "now" experience. Nothing more! Everything else doesn't matter. And we keep living like tomorrow, or next week, or next year, or when this or that happens, when I can, if I can, as though that will be the right time. If you are so fortunate to be here tomorrow morning, all you've got is one more NOW! PRESENT! So when is the time to start? **DON'T WAIT UNTIL YOU FEEL INSPIRED**. You do it now. I don't care how you feel. When is the time to reconcile your differences with others? Now – tonight! Get it done! When is the time for you to passionately chase your goals and say that's it; I surrender to what's required of me. There is no turning back! I'm in the game for keeps. You can't knock me out. You can knock me down, but you can't knock me out, because as long as I can get up one more time, you have not beaten me. And if you were to beat me today, you have not conquered me because you cannot beat my spirit. Now go and live your life. Would it make a difference? Yes, it would make a difference.

Do you have the inherent power to change, or will your old attitudes of mind continue to block you from becoming the magnificent creature that you were designed to become? Re-invent yourself! Now go and do the work required and expect to be victorious in the pursuit of your dreams. Only you can decide if it's worth the effort. I can only tell you, from personal experience, that it is. And, as always in life, the choice is uniquely yours and so will the outcome of that choice be uniquely of your own fashioning.

**"Thank you for having the courage
to take this journey with me."**

*George Zalucki*

# *Personal Insights I've Gained*

# *Your Life Is A Motion Picture Where You Get To Be The Producer, The Director, The Writer, And The Actor As Well.*
## *You are Totally Responsible For Winning Or Losing The Academy Award!*

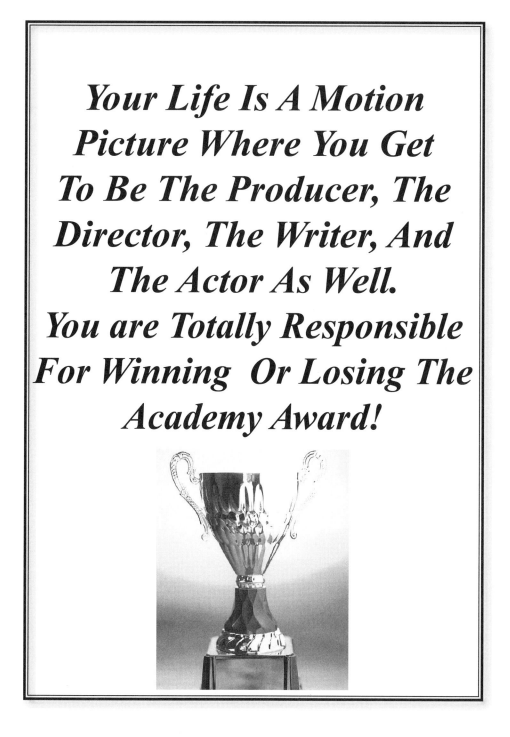

# Section 6
# The Workbook

# <u>*Leadership Training*</u>

Rate yourself 1-10 for each of these traits and work to increase your score!

_____Mission Driven – Focus on the objective

_____Personal Initiative

_____Self Confidence

_____Creative – Become a problem solver

_____Enthusiasm – and the ability to transmit it to others

_____Character – Does not bend his or her principles

_____Courage – To lead when the going gets tough

_____Uncommon work ethic

_____Tolerance

_____Ability to cooperate in a spirit of harmony

_____Good Listener

_____Charisma – A quality you develop

_____Trustworthy – People will follow someone they trust

_____Mastery over greed

_____Mastery of Ego

_____Servants Mentality

_____Conviction – You've got to totally believe you will win

_____Integrity – Be honest in all dealings

_____Uncommon Perseverance - All winners possess this quality!

Name:_____

Date_____

*"Winners are not born, they are developed! G.Z.*

# *A Financial Reality Test*

Write down your gross monthly income     _____

Deduct your taxes      -_____

You now have your net disposable income   _____

Now list your expenses:

Mortgage or rent per month     _____

Utilities, gas and electric     _____

All Insurances     _____

Auto, life, home, health

Auto payments, lease, gas, maintance     _____

Telephones     _____

Clothing family     _____

Personal care     _____

School expenses     _____

Gifts     _____

Cable TV     _____

Medical costs     _____

Home maintance     _____

Food expense monthly     _____

Credit card monthly payments     _____

Entertinment –vacations – travel     _____

Charity or Church donations     _____

Savings and investments     _____

          $$_____

**The true story is what is on this last line**

**What is left here is determining your financial future!!!!**

# *My Personal Goal Sheet*

**Yesterday is gone forever!  The time to win is now!**

List 5 goals you will accomplish!

1_____

_____

_____._____

_____

_____

_____

_____By_____

2._____

_____

_____

_____

_____

_____By_____

3._____

_____

_____

_____

_____By_____

4._____

_____

_____

_____

_____

_____By_____

5._____

_____

_____

_____

_____

_____By_____

**In life there is only the moment you are in. And so it will be for all your tomorrows.**

**So, declare your intentions to achieve these written goals. Visualize, Believe, Plan, and work the plan until they are achieved!**

# *What Motivates Me?*

**Rate each motivator on a scale from 1-10.**
**The higher the rating the stronger the power to motivate.**

_____Money
_____Appreciation
_____Recognition
_____Serving Others
_____Being Loved
_____Sex
_____Power
_____Family
_____Financial Security
_____Emotional Security
_____Competition
_____Belonging
_____Spiritual Well Being
_____Other_____
_____Other_____

**Now list your top 5 motivators from the above:**

1._____
2._____
3._____
4._____
5._____

## Now list the strongest two from the five:

1._____

2._____

Do these possess enough power to sustain you enroute to your goals?

Now list 4 emotions you are feeling right now?

1._____

2._____

3._____

4._____

What are these emotions telling you?

_____

_____

_____

_____

_____

_____

_____

_____

_____

_____

_____

_____

# *What De-Motivates me?*

Rate each de-motivator on a scale of 1-10.
The higher the rating the stronger the power to de-motivate.


_____**Doubt**

_____**Confusion**

_____**Disappointment**

_____**Frustration**

_____**Offended**

_____**Tired**

_____**Bored**

_____**Guilt**

_____**Overwhelm**

_____**Worry**

_____**Inferior**

_____**Humiliation**

_____**Rejection**

_____**Jealousy**

_____**Shame**

_____**Incompetence**

_____**Ridicule**

_____**Embarrassed**

_____**Ugly**

_____**Overweight**

_____**Hate**

_____**Past Failures**

**Now list your top 5 De-motivators**

1._____
2._____
3._____
4._____
5._____

Do these have enough negative power to prevent you from achieving your goals?  Have they done so in the past?

List 5 possessions or experiences that you missed out on, lost because of these de-motivators.

1._____
2._____
3._____
4._____
5._____

## *Your Power Dynamic*

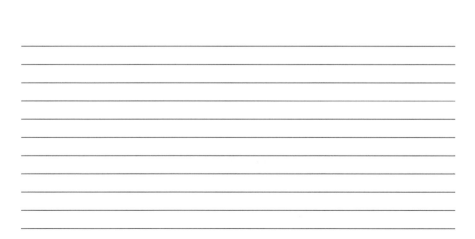

# YOUR POWER DYNAMIC
### *Now List Your Opposing Motivators and De-Motivators*

| Motivator | Rating | De-motivator | Rating |
|---|---|---|---|
| 1. | _____ | 1. | _____ |
| 2. | _____ | 2. | _____ |
| 3. | _____ | 3. | _____ |
| 4. | _____ | 4. | _____ |
| 5. | _____ | 5. | _____ |
| Total | _____ | Total | _____ |

*What do you think you need to understand, learn more about, or deal with in order to increase your motivation power and decrease your de-motivating power drain?*

_____

_____

_____

_____

_____

_____

_____

_____

_____

_____

# *Dissatisfaction Analysis*

It is important to get in touch with the real (not repressed) level of **DISSATISFACTION** with categories listed below.

## Reality Inventory
### A time for honesty

| My life Now | Present status | Rate 1-10 dissatisfaction | What needs to change? | My committed goal |
|---|---|---|---|---|
| Job/Career | | | | |
| Income | | | | |
| Savings | | | | |
| Investments | | | | |
| Housing | | | | |
| Car | | | | |
| Clothing | | | | |

What do you need to change to raise your **SATISFACTION** level?

_____

_____

_____

_____

# *Dissatisfaction Analysis 2*

## Reality Inventory
### A time for honesty

| My life Now | Present status | Rate 1-10 dissatisfaction | What needs to change? | My committed goal |
|---|---|---|---|---|
| Health | | | | |
| Vacations | | | | |
| Relationships | | | | |
| Retirement | | | | |
| Liabilities | | | | |
| Assets | | | | |
| Net worth | | | | |

## What Are Your Choices?

List options or ideas to increase your **SATISFACTION** level?

_____

_____

_____

_____

# *The Time is Now*

The work sheet that follows is designed to guide you to better time management by 1) Reviewing your current methods and procedures; and 2) Enabling you to pinpoint those areas needing improvement. Here is how to use it:

Go through the 25 items on this page and check off each point as to whether it is satisfactory or could stand improvement,

1. Planning time for the task _____
2. Setting deadlines _____
3. Making changes fast _____
4. Adjusting to increased workload _____
5. Preventing duplicated work _____
6. Spending available time _____
7. Redistributing the workload _____
8. Getting rid of accumulated tasks _____
9. Avoiding low priority interruptions _____
10. Handling disliked tasks _____
11. Using odd moments productively_____
12. Working with your upline_____
13. Spending time with distributors _____
14. Delegation techniques_____
15. Use of meeting time _____
16. Speaking skills _____
17. Organizing reference materials _____
18. Organizing your To Do List_____
19. Telephone practices_____

20. Outlining skills that need improvement _____

21. Reading and study time_____

22. Habit analysis_____

23. Making use of my best abilities _____

24. Travel time _____

25. Working at home _____

Satisfactory Total_____

Improvement needed total_____

# *What Has Procrastination Cost Me?*

This is the time for truth. You see procrastination is a 100% commitment to failure!!!

List 10 things you have accomplished or achieved success in, and 10 losses you have sustained because of procrastination. What has procrastination cost you?

## Wins

1. _____
2. _____
3. _____
4. _____
5. _____
6. _____
7. _____
8. _____
9. _____
10. _____

## Losses

1. _____
2. _____
3. _____
4. _____
5. _____
6. _____
7. _____
8. _____
9. _____
10. _____

# *What must I include, improve, or overcome on my journey to success?*

# Notes

# Notes

# Notes

# Notes

# Notes